Living for Real—

Koukyotos

OLIVE DRAB

Pom-Poms

Kori Yates

CROSSBOOKS
PUBLISHING

CrossBooks™
A Division of LifeWay
1663 Liberty Drive
Bloomington, IN 47403
www.crossbooks.com
Phone: 1-866-879-0502

First published by CrossBooks 5/26/2011

ISBN: 978-1-6150-7878-3 (e)
ISBN: 978-1-6150-7879-0 (hc)

Library of Congress Control Number: 2011929330

Printed in the United States of America

This book is printed on acid-free paper.

Dedication

This book is dedicated to Jesus, my Savior, who saw something to love in me, and to my own cheerleader, Kyle Yates.

Acknowledgements

As with any project I have ever undertaken, this could not have been done on my own. I am thankful for friends and family who have molded and encouraged me along this journey in life. I am thankful for my brother, Lee Whatley, who could take graphics in my head and make them come to life on a computer screen, and for Linda Yezak and my writing group in Nacogdoches, Texas who believed I could succeed in my quest and challenged me to become better. I am also thankful for my battle buddies – those military wives who have held me up and guided me along the way – most especially Beth Sanders who gave her heart and time as she read, listened, and prayed many hours for this very thing.

Contents

Introduction

I refuse to simply be a survivor. The word itself seems to conjure up feelings of drudgery and complacency, both of which are unacceptable to me. I am a firm believer that God has much more planned for my life than being satisfied with the status quo.

As military wives, we sometimes get caught up in survival mode. We hope to hold on until the next Permanent Change of Station (PCS) or the end of a deployment, believing that somehow the next phase will be better or easier than the last. This is not what God intended for us. We are not here by accident. This military-wife life is no surprise to God. He planned long ago where He would have our husbands serve, and He knew even then that we would be involved. He had a plan for us too.

We are here for a purpose and a calling, not to survive. In every step of my life, I want to know what He has planned for me. I never want to miss a moment or an opportunity. My ultimate objective is to give everything I have to the calling and life God planned for me. I've determined that being the kind of military wife that God called me to be requires skills that I haven't used in years—and some I'm pretty sure I've never had.

I am a cheerleader with olive drab pom-poms, but this is no teeny-bopper cutesy assignment. This kind of cheerleading involves fierce competition, takes true athletic skill, and hopefully includes some cute clothes along the way.

I never was a very good cheerleader. Lack of rhythm was my downfall. My last attempt to be on a squad happened in the first grade. I loved the "outfit," and had a great time, but to say the least, I was not wholly successful. My coordination and rhythm abilities have been the topic of more than one family joke.

My dream was to be a Dallas Cowboy Cheerleader, but that dream was never realized. We should all be thankful! In this initial attempt at "cheerleaderdom," I learned that I might not have the physical gifts to make me successful, but I do have the heart.

God has brought me full circle. I married a soldier, and now I *am* a cheerleader. Not the caliber of a Dallas Cowboy cheerleader, but one nonetheless. My pom-poms are olive drab, and I've come to believe and understand that this is exactly what God planned for me. And it requires no rhythm!

This life I live is not necessarily what I had envisioned. At one time, I wanted to coach high school basketball, or even try my hand at being a United States senator. When I was four years old, I wanted to be a sales clerk at Sears, mostly because the Sears parking lot in our town was on top of the building, and an escalator led down to the store. Who wouldn't want to work in such a cool place? Apparently, God had other things planned. I never expected this adventure.

I don't walk the steps of the capitol and make decisions that change history. I don't experience the thrill and excitement of leading a team to victory. I don't even get to park on top of the building. But in my own little part of God's great big plan, I make a difference because I'm exactly where He wants me to be. I currently serve as the president of my husband's fan club. I've always enjoyed being in charge, and this is my chance. I grab my olive drab pom-poms and cheer him on.

In addition to having such an awesome job as my husband's cheerleader, I also know, beyond a shadow of a doubt, that I have a personal calling from God. Just like cheerleaders who are responsible for cheering at the games, but also for participating in outside competitions,

God has more for me than bouncing on the sidelines of my husband's career. Sometimes it's a struggle to find God's plan, but the possibilities are endless.

I've had this military-wife assignment for a few years, and it's been both a joy and a challenge. I love the military's traditions and standards—the pride—the history. I love the camaraderie of the military family and the adventure of military life. I'm challenged by the same things as others: long hours, deployments, field time, etc. But, I refuse to let negative experiences overshadow great ones. I choose to cheer on the team—*my* team—until God leads my husband down another path.

Some may be skeptical and expect this book to be about living our lives through our husbands. It's much more than that. This book is about finding our part in our husbands' careers, but it's even more about learning what God desires us as individuals to be and do. Military life is no reason to discard God's will for our lives. We need to discover our calling and realize that God planned for it to coexist with military life.

So, are you with me? Take up your pom-poms and cheer with all your might for the marriage, the man, and the calling that God has given you. Join me as we seek God through *the adventure of our lives* as military wives, praying in the meantime that God will sustain us and our marriages. We'll strive to fulfill God's calling in our lives, and be stronger when we finish than when we started. This is the opportunity of a lifetime. Hang on, chicks! We're going to rock—rhythm or no rhythm!

Chapter One

Part of the Game

The stadium gates are open. Handing off our recently purchased tickets, we enter high school's most hallowed ground. Summer's heat bears down, but the smell of booster club hotdogs on the grill entices us onward. With food in hand and cokes dripping with sweat, we mount the bleachers. The field with its precision hash marks comes into view, and the perfume of fresh-cut grass overtakes us. The school band's off-key warm-up tickles our ears and starts the adrenaline rush anticipating the inevitable battle that will take place on the field. The fight song will soon be played by heart and sung with unending devotion by those around us.

We search for a seat and pray only to find a small piece of metal covered with shade where we can rest from the last days of summer. Dressed impeccably in their uniforms, the cheerleaders prepare the spray-painted banner that will welcome our team onto the field. The banner-waving flag team joins in this contest of school spirit, not to be outdone by the faithful die-hards with painted faces, rattling cowbells in one hand, and half-eaten hotdogs in the other. At long last, our day has culminated to this very moment. The home team is proclaimed from the loudspeakers, and our heroes join us from their pep rally in the locker room. Through the eruption of excitement, we realize one thing. Friday night football has arrived.

The football players are the focal point of the exhibition, but what individuals and organizations contribute makes the game what it is. From parents working the booster club concession stand, to flute players with school songs ingrained in their minds, they have all come to play a part in the game. No longer is the spectacle just a bunch of guys wearing pads and running into each other. The game becomes a demonstration of school pride in multiple areas. In this one event, people who rarely engage in the school's halls become a united front to the world. This is high school football.

Cheerleaders, for all their beauty-queen reputation, are a part of this event as well. Irreplaceable. Crucial. Necessary. These are not words often used to describe them when discussing a football game. Truth be told, they are rarely mentioned at all, and yet somehow it is difficult to imagine a game without them.

Friday night football, especially in our home state of Texas, is the highlight of most towns, hands down. These are the glory days of high school. The Saturday newspaper tells the story with glowing reports. Players' photos are printed across the front page of the sports section, along with game statistics containing touchdowns, first downs, tackles, and possessions. These exciting stories of athleticism and strategy seem to have little, if anything, to do with the cheerleaders.

And yet, after watching many of these games, I've come to the conclusion that cheerleaders are vital components of the game. Based upon school tradition and expectation, cheerleaders have different responsibilities—like leading the team onto the field, or creating an "alley" through which the team can run, sometimes even using spray-painted banners to add to the excitement. They provide the pom-pom waving, cartwheeling, back-flipping ambience that makes those in the bleachers want to stand and shout.

They continue with this enthusiasm throughout the entire game and sometimes even into overtime. These passionate and dedicated followers bring a certain excitement to the game that would otherwise be sorely missed.

Tasks vary from one squad to the next, but one common duty stands above all others and is performed by every cheerleader, regardless of skill. This assignment is clear; inspire the crowd no matter what the scoreboard reads, and inspire the team to fight, regardless of the odds. Cheerleaders are not actual physical participants in the battle. They do, however, provide support and encouragement to those around them.

This task is one only the cheerleader can fill. A coach's pat on the back and parents applauding in the stands are great, but they don't compare to girls bouncing on the sidelines—especially in high school. Not only does the cheerleader assure the player that he's supported, regardless of his ability or the outcome of the game, she also inspires others to do the same. This, my friend, is vital for football success.

Irreplaceable

Military wives fulfill a similar role and have very similar outcomes. Just like cheerleaders, we never score a touchdown, and tackling someone is not even a remote thought (well, not in most instances anyway). Our names are not called to receive medals and awards. The newspapers do not list us as hometown heroes, and our adventures abroad are often overlooked. Even to buy groceries, we must show a card that says we're married to men in uniforms. Nonetheless, we are irreplaceable to at least one player, and therefore, we're vital to the team's success. Just like cheerleaders on the football field, the game would not be the same without us.

Imagine with me that we are the cheerleaders. I know this is a challenge for some of us who lack true physical skill and have rarely, if ever, worn anything similar to one of their uniforms, but stay with me. Our husbands are the players. They remain on the field for the duration of the game. Sometimes they're victorious, sometimes they're battered and bruised, and sometimes they experience both. Their names are on the jerseys, scouts come to watch them play, and they're the ones who receive the accolades.

We can all imagine the scenario even if we've never lived it—literally. This is the perfect example of our military-wife life. We all have times when we feel we're just the frou-frou part of our husbands' careers—not a necessity, more like a decoration. Our only contribution is to stand beside him and smile sweetly. At some point in our husbands' careers, we actually thought our role as military wives might simply be one of a hood ornament or prized trophy, whose sole purpose is to smile and be dusted periodically. We've all been there.

We all know, beyond a shadow of a doubt, the military is never going to ask our opinions about where we want to move, to which unit our husbands should be attached, or even what hours we think our husbands might be able to work. Most of the things that happen are simply beyond our control; we have no choice but to hang on for the ride.

But there is so much more! We are all fundamental components to our husbands and families. God started this idea as far back as Adam and Eve (Genesis 2:4-24). Adam was created first. Following his creation, God in His infinite wisdom decided it was not good that Adam be alone. He decided to "make a helper suitable for him."

Of all the animals God brought for Adam to name, none was a "suitable helper" for him, so God caused Adam to sleep and formed a woman from his rib. Like me, you may have learned this story in Sunday school, but I'd like to share what recently caught my attention.

First, God allowed Adam to meet every other creature made so he could understand his needs. I'd always remembered Adam and Eve being created one immediately following the other, and yet this was not the case. Whether there was a difference of hours or minutes, Adam needed to see that he was lacking a "helper." God provided exactly what Adam needed when He introduced Adam to Eve.

Second, although Adam was asleep during Eve's creation, when he saw her, he immediately knew that she was a part of him. Initially, love at first sight came to mind, but I believe this was much more than love.

Beyond a shadow of a doubt, Adam knew this was who God had made for him. This woman was his helper. She would be a part of him for life. In this union, they did become one flesh.

Our marriages today are no different. Granted, we were not formed from our husbands' ribs, but we did become one flesh in the union of marriage. Sin's initiation into the world—as well as mountains of discussion—took place before Paul was led centuries later to explain our individual roles in this union.

In Ephesians 5:22-33, Paul explains the roles of husbands and wives in a marriage. He brings out a point that connects us back to Genesis. Paul illustrates this union by comparing the husbands to Christ (the head) and the wives to the church or body of Christ. The idea of unity in marriage becomes painfully clear in that one truly needs the other to function.

If we follow Paul's comparison, we see that the husband is the head and the wife is the body. Imagine with me how successful the husband (head) would be without the wife (body). An interesting thought, I know. The head would be completely dysfunctional. Although it would have the mental ability to accomplish some things, it would have no appendages or heart to do so.

Now before we get too heady over our husbands' reliance upon us for success, we must remember that the body is not much good without the head either. Years ago, when family came to visit, my husband's grandmother would capture a choice chicken and chop off its head, a grotesque process seldom resulting in the bird's immediate death. Through the power of its nerves, the headless chicken was still able to run around the yard. From this comes the saying "running around like a chicken with his head cut off."

In my reading and understanding of these Scriptures, I can totally relate to the bird. I would look much like that chicken should something ever happen to my wonderful husband. The permanency of the marriage union should become much clearer. God has designed us to become one. Apart from God separating us through death, this union is designed to be inseparable by man without significant injury to the parties involved. Bottom line—as wives, we're irreplaceable and necessary to our husbands.

Our Role

Shocking, I know, to see that we are so vitally important. Even the army has lately figured out that a strong family makes a much stronger soldier.

This is not rocket science. We wives have known this for years. We have desired to make our homes a safe and peaceful place for our families. We've longed to make each house a home where our family can be just that . . . a family. We've come to understand that each individual in our family is much more successful *outside* the home if we're all working together *inside* the home. Our husbands need a sanctuary where they can rest and be cared for so they can be successful. We understand this concept, but we sometimes lose sight of the fact that *we* are an integral part in making it happen.

Some of the things we experience in normal military life are unique to us, but many of the things we go through have been experienced by most military wives . . . more than once. For instance, our nomadic lifestyle. We move. Some of us move more frequently than others, and some receive more advanced notice, but almost every military wife I've encountered has moved at least once.

Moving is never easy, but it's a great example of teamwork and division of assignments in marriage. Parts of this move can be handled by the wife—like the walk-through by the moving company or purchasing food for the movers. We can find a home at our new location, and sometimes we can even sign for it. Our husbands have duties they must perform, as well. They must process off of post/base and sign transportation paperwork. Add in all the "little" things like supervising our children, dividing up shipments, registering at new schools, or checking into DEERS, teamwork becomes necessary for success.

At times, one spouse may take on more responsibility than the other, but the point is the same, regardless. We are in this together;

neither spouse can accomplish this task successfully without assistance and support from the other. God has given us exactly what we need—each other. All of us are essential to the success of the venture . . . wives included. We're a part of the game.

Husband and wife must be in the journey together. We're a team, and a team that is not united is not victorious. Jesus pointed this out specifically in Matthew 12:25 when He said, "Every kingdom divided against itself will be ruined, and every city or household divided against itself will not stand." Our goals and objectives need to match. Our hearts need to be as one. We must learn to stand together or we will not stand at all. This simple point reiterates our importance in this endeavor.

Our contribution reaches far beyond a simple move and expands into everyday life. Whether we realize it or not, we become exactly what God intended for us to be—our husbands' partners in this quest we call "life." What higher calling is there than to be doing exactly what God called us to do? We help with everything from meals and house chores to listening and encouraging our husbands, although listening and encouraging may be considered more important.

At times, relationship building may take place thousands of miles a part. Whether in the same room or via e-mail, the conversation is just as important. In an ideal world, this gesture will be reciprocated, but realize that this may not always be possible. Time, as well as other factors, may play into the scenario. During our marriages, each spouse will have times when giving back is a challenge, whether this is due to time constraints, emotional challenges, struggles with other things like work, or the inability to communicate when the timing is convenient for us. We'll find that more often than not, one spouse gives more than the other. Preferably this happens at different times.

In most marriages, everyone takes turns giving a little extra. It's normal for that role to be reversed, and then reversed again, depending on the situation. Remember, this is not about keeping score and figuring out who gives more. Marriage is like most relationships in the fact that it becomes more meaningful when we are more concerned for another than we are for ourselves.

Through these experiences and conversations, we become our husband's support and partner, not just the sidekick that follows along behind. We become not only his cheerleader, but the president of his fan club. We begin to see that through all of his faults, he is exactly what God planned for us. We become thankful to be a part of his calling by fulfilling our own.

The Covenant

Have no fear . . . the challenges will come. Some days our husbands will make us angry. Some days they will not do things the way we think they should. Some days we may even wonder who in the world these men are that we married, but do not forget that these are the men God called us to marry. And even if we did not marry them based on a calling we felt, we have now entered a covenant relationship.

This covenant binds us together as only God can. He explains this as far back as the time of creation when the first union was formed. "Then the Lord God made a woman from the rib he had taken out of the man, and he brought her to the man. The man said, 'This is now bone of my bone and flesh of my flesh; she shall be called 'woman' for she was taken out of man.' For this reason a man will leave his father and mother and be united to his wife, and they will become one flesh"(Genesis 2:22-24).

Many of us may have heard this Scripture read on our wedding day. We're reminded that the union we call marriage makes us one in the eyes of God, whether or not we feel it at the time. This is our covenant for life. God will honor our commitment and our faithfulness to the covenant we have made.

I heard the marriage relationship explained as the single most important relationship on the planet. It is the only relationship God made that was a picture, albeit a small and imperfect one, of His relationship with His people.

With this comparison we carry a heavy responsibility, but also a great privilege. Through marriage, we have a chance to share Christ with people by being an example of who God designed us to be. We're only responsible for our part in that and our husband for his. We simply need to do exactly what God called us to do, even when imperfections arise, as they surely will. We must learn to use the challenges of our marriage to grow and draw closer to our Savior.

As we all realized, either prior to marriage or immediately thereafter, our husbands will not be perfect (neither will we) throughout the lifetime of this relationship. When challenged through this relationship, our best bet is to look for the things he does well and encourage him. Be a good sounding board for the questions and decisions he encounters. Share our opinion and perspective when appropriate. In the end, honor God by ultimately submitting to our husbands' decisions. And pray.

Of all the things we can do to be his cheerleader, prayer is by far the most important and most powerful. If we struggle in the cheerleader role, if our husband is challenged and we cannot help physically, if questions and decisions arise that need clarification, if our relationship is not what it could be, or if we have the most awesome marriage and everything is going great—our answer is always to hit our knees in prayer. Take the struggles, questions, frustrations, hopes, thankfulness, and joy and give it all to the Father. We must share our hearts with Him as we strive to be what our families need, but more importantly, what God wants us to be.

James talks about the importance of prayer, regardless of circumstances (James 5:13-16). We are to pray whether we're troubled, happy, sick, or struggling with sin. In closing he graciously reminds us to "confess your sins to each other and pray for each other so that you may be healed. The prayer of a righteous man is powerful and effective" (James 5:16). I, personally, have a difficult time thinking of myself as "righteous," but God apparently sees me that way regardless.

Righteousness is not a matter of being perfect, it is a matter of being justified. We became righteous when we asked Christ into our lives, and we continue in righteousness as we strive to be more like Him.

We will be made complete in righteousness when we see the Father face-to-face. It's a state in which Christians live and a goal for which Christians strive. As Christians, we are all considered righteous. James points out that our prayers—the prayers of the righteous—are powerful and effective. What an awesome thought!

Prayer can change the world. So changing a situation or our marriage is not a very far reach. Realizing that we have such power at our fingertips and using it—talk about rockin' cheerleaders. We will be the bomb! What cheerleader wouldn't desire to talk to the Master of the entire universe and change the specific plays of the game, or even the total outcome? The possibilities are endless. We could take a high school team to the state championship or an NFL team to the Super Bowl—and win! Even closer to home, we could take a mediocre player whose only hope is to warm the bench and lead him to the all-state team. We accomplish all of this simply because we stopped to have a conversation and develop a relationship with the living God. We have now become a vital component—an irreplaceable participant in the game.

In the vast military world, it doesn't take much for a spouse to feel very small and insignificant. Our husbands consider their jobs very important. With this weight of responsibility, the phone calls come late at night, the hours are long, and the deployments can be frequent. Whether or not they like the military, they spend a vast amount of time fulfilling the job expected of them. As wives, we can begin to feel like we're only awarded time left over. Yet, we cover everything on the home front from cleaning the house and taking care of the children to balancing the checkbook and managing home improvements/repairs.

Whether we feel like a priority in our husbands' lives or not, we are a priority to God. Paul gives us all some encouragement and a simple reminder in Colossians 3:23-24 where he writes, "Whatever you do, work at it with all of your heart, as working for the Lord, and not for men, since you know that you will receive an inheritance from the Lord as a reward. It is the Lord Christ you are serving." How this one verse can change our attitudes! Reminding ourselves that everything we do is for Christ's glory and as service to Him makes the struggle seem far more worthwhile and the job much easier.

Perspective

Step back and take in the view. Cheerleaders may be standing on the sidelines, but their view is amazing. People would pay big bucks to stand in their Nike shoes. Look how close they are to the action. Even sportscasters wish they could often stand in a cheerleader's shoes because they can see the plays in detail, as well as the attitude and personality of each player. This is a definite advantage.

Cheerleaders can catch a glimpse of the coach's attitude by the expression on his face or overhearing what he says. Cheerleaders see how players interact, and by hearing press conversations to chats at the water cooler, they become aware of players' strengths and weaknesses. All of these details combine to prove one point. Cheerleaders are highly valuable because of their unique perspective.

This applies to us. We see the players (and their wives) at different events. If we open our eyes, we can watch their interaction, as well as the "coach's" direction. We have a great vantage point and can help our husbands as they share excitement and frustration about what is going on around them. We're able to provide a different perspective. Remember in these times, though, that each person (players and spouses) is a part of the puzzle and God has placed them all here for a reason.

We and our husbands will find that the military, like every other organization, has people who are easy to work with, and then there are the "others." Attitude and perspective are vital.

As cheerleaders, remember that we are important to the game, but we nonetheless stand on the sidelines. We can't decide to jump on the field and tackle anyone, much as we would like to at times (although it would be quite painful considering we have no pads or helmet). Playing the game is not our responsibility. That job belongs to our husbands.

We are not even expected to coach the team. We must learn as much about the game as we can and provide perspective, support, encouragement, and connection with the fans. This is our job. We should never, I repeat, *never* decide to play on the offensive line. The soreness of being run over will last for days, not to mention the fact that our loving husbands will have to walk out on the field and carry us off. Life is better when we fulfill the role we've been given. We must fulfill the call God has placed on *our* lives, and let our husbands answer *their* call. In the end we will be an unstoppable team!

This unique perspective we offer also allows us to be the primary liaison between the game and the bleachers. We've fulfilled this role many times. Often, we're their connection with our community, our church, and even our families. We keep the bleachers abreast of the game, and when the game is finished we let our husbands know who was there to watch.

People in the bleachers also play important roles in the game. Serving as the booster club—parents, grandparents, and other family members religiously support our husbands through everything from phone calls to care packages. Our children fulfill the role of those faithful die-hards with their faces painted and half-eaten hotdogs. The bleachers are filled with fans from our churches and communities who have paid big bucks to be here and sit on the home team side. They're all excited—sometimes even enough to do the wave when the team needs a little extra motivation. We are their connection to the game, keeping them engaged, informed, and focused.

The liaison role in real-life can mean anything from calling our mothers-in-law to give them updates to sharing prayer requests with our Sunday school classes. We keep our children connected through interaction with our spouses when they're home, and phone calls and videos when they are gone.

Our liaison role also stretches to our communities where we let people know, even through everyday conversation, that what our husbands do is important, and that men and women protect and serve our country around the world every day. We don't blow our own horn or tout our husbands as the only hero. But when they cannot be there to connect with the important people in our lives, we have the opportunity to help. This role is fulfilled many times without even thinking about it, but it is a strategic play of the game that must be replayed over and over—connecting the bleachers with the field.

Bottom line is that as our husbands' cheerleaders, we are an irreplaceable part of the game, their partners in all of life through a covenant we made both to them and to God. We also have a calling all our own in this adventure, and we're equipped to fulfill it as God would have us do.

Our unique perspective is one that can be very advantageous to us and to our husbands if we use it in the proper way. We are able to share insight and be a great sounding board. Our position is also one that many would envy as we stand so close to the game itself. We are a vital part of their world—a part of them. We are part of the game!

No doubt, some may have come to the end of this chapter thinking that their only role in life is to bounce on the sidelines of their husbands' careers. Some may even be tempted to put this book down believing that there is more to life than waving pom-poms and talking to our mothers-in-law. Have no fear, I completely agree.

The desire to write this book began when I started noticing military wives living from one deployment to the next or one duty station to the next, hoping for something better than where they were. Some became discouraged and challenged by military life because they had yet to find contentment and purpose in the place God had put them. They didn't realize or had forgotten that God had so much more for them in every location along the way than a cute uniform and Friday night games.

What does He have for us? What else is He calling us to be and do? These are the exact questions God would like us to ask. So ... let's ask! Jump in with me, see what other stunts He has in store for us, and train and challenge ourselves to be the true athlete He made us to be!

Chapter Two

Stunts

Cheerleading is now recognized as a sport—no longer entirely dependent on great looks and popularity. The NCAA has even debated adding it to their athletic repertoire alongside football, baseball, and soccer. This is leaps and bounds beyond the popularity contest I remember from high school. I was a basketball/volleyball player then and considered myself a "real" athlete.

Cheerleaders, on the other hand, were simply the girls with lots of admirers and little skill. Tryouts displayed this truth in action. While students filled the bleachers, these young ladies dressed in black and gold outfits of their own making individually entered the gymnasium and demonstrated skills acquired through the arduous training of the previous month. Most attempted to do some sort of cartwheel or round-off, although a few possessed acrobatic ability. One girl even ran to the center of the gymnasium, and attempting to do a cartwheel, placed both hands on the floor and hopped her feet over. I thought she had no chance of winning. But you know what? She did! She was quite popular and very pretty. I was amazed.

Since that time, cheerleading has changed from a pom-pom waving beauty contest to a competitive sport. In most cities, cheerleading classes are readily available for girls as young as four or five years old and competitions abound. Girls today have some skill! They can do the basic splits and cartwheels—and a whole lot more. They perform amazing stunts. These girls run, lift weights, and train for specific stunts, all to become even better at what they do. They grow in strength and coordination as they get older, resulting in cheerleaders who are much more than a pretty face in a cute skirt. I love to watch them. I mean, how cool would it be to be able to flip like that or have someone throw me in the air while I flipped over?

How much easier would it be to have classes on being a military wife prior to actually jumping in! We would like to have had some practice or prior training before joining the big leagues. But in this game, we were first round draft picks with absolutely no play time behind us. We went from no experience at all to the National Football League. True, classes like Army Family Teambuilding (AFTB) are offered to those engaged to military personnel, or even civilians for that matter. We had access to such things, but I would seriously doubt many of us took the opportunity. Surely it is more fun to just jump right in!

Military wives, just like cheerleaders, do amazing things. We are much more than "a pretty face in a cute skirt." We help take care of our families, hold jobs, fulfill expectations as military wives, and still keep our sanity—mostly. We do our jobs—our amazing stunts—whether the ones we love are with us or in a distant land. I'm always impressed when I leave the house on time, my clothes matching, both kids in tow, and my cell phone in hand. My husband is usually impressed at these moments as well—they're not frequent. I usually forget the cell phone and remember the kids. At least I have my priorities in order.

When performed over and over, though, these everyday achievements become an amazing accomplishment in themselves. As we finish a day, a week, or a year, we should look back and see all that we have done . . . all that God has helped us do. Remember just the little things, like getting the kids up and to school on time, or buying what we actually needed at the grocery store, are great accomplishments. We have succeeded in much, though some days it may seem highly insignificant.

Service

In addition to these normal family accomplishments, we do so much more. Many of us volunteer for organizations both on and off post. Some of us volunteer time at our child's school. We jump right in and work with the spouses' organization for our husbands' unit, teach a Sunday school class or Bible study at church, and do multiple "extra-curricular activities" outside the little world of our families. Stop and think about all the phone calls made, the potluck dishes cooked, the decorations we've helped hang, the paperwork we've assisted in completing, and the time spent doing something for others.

Volunteer time over months and years becomes difficult to track or even fathom. The military has attempted to track some of these volunteer hours through a volunteer management system. Although moderately successful, we've found that some hours will never be counted, and the vast plethora of activities is astounding. We have contributed much to our families, our installations, and the communities in which we have lived. We have made a difference simply by having a heart for helping others.

Added to these awesome accomplishments, many of us have full or part-time paying jobs, where our skills are varied as well. The number and types of positions we fill are amazing, from customer service level positions to highly qualified executives. We arrive on time, do the job asked of us and sometimes more. We stay a little late if necessary, help others around us, and even volunteer at times for duties outside of our normal job description.

A great number of us do an awesome job and have learned the required skills through on-the-job training. I am a huge proponent of education and actually love school, and it would have been much easier to learn my occupation if I'd taken a class, but I found that most of the things I've learned have been through trial and error, or simply by asking someone for help. I believe this has actually helped me grow. These volunteer and paid opportunities have taught us new things about ourselves and allowed us to serve outside our homes.

Some military wives go far beyond what some of us could think or imagine. They become social reform advocates, chief executive officers, and politicians. They hold any number of titles, but their actions are more noticeable to the public at large. Many of them are spurred on by a challenge they faced, a problem they desired to solve, a dream they chased and caught. They have accomplished awesome things and still seem to maintain their priorities of God and family. I'm awed by what God has called these women to do and their zeal in following that call.

Military wives are no different with regard to our service than most other wives. We do what is necessary and then we do a little bit more. We are wives, moms, leaders, organizers, supervisors, laborers, hosts, servants. We have many more hats than the one we wear as a military wife. Many of us accomplish great and honorable things everyday without even thinking about it. We are compassionate, thoughtful, sacrificial . . . and remarkable.

The Calling

No matter where we serve, one thing stands out above the rest—God has other callings for us besides "military wife." God does not want us to simply sit by and wait as the world, and our lives, pass us by. He has given us a purpose. He has a plan for *our* lives. In God's eyes, each one of us is special. He desires for us to share an intimate relationship with Him (one-on-One), giving each of us gifts and abilities that we may not even know we have. He has drawn out a path for our lives with milestones along the way that He desires for us to reach. By tapping into the power and strength He's given us, He desires for us to change the world. This may mean the entire world, or it may mean the world around us. Either way, it is a divine plan just for us.

In Matthew 10:46-52, Bartimaeus, a blind man sitting on the side of the road outside of Jericho, was begging alms from passers-by when he heard that Jesus of Nazareth was coming. He began to shout, asking Jesus to have mercy on him. The people around him kept telling him to be quiet, but Jesus heard him. He told the disciples to bring him. The disciples went to the man and said my favorite words of the story, "Cheer up! On your feet! He's calling you" (Mark 10:49). Bartimaeus' reaction? He threw off his coat, jumped to his feet, and went to Jesus.

How awesome that Jesus called *him*, an insignificant beggar, personally? Many other people were obviously around, as well as noises from the city, and yet Jesus still heard him. Not only did He hear Bartimaeus, He responded. Jesus called him.

The words of the disciples are just as true today. The Bible is talking to us! "Cheer up! Get on your feet! He's calling you." He is calling me. We simply have to get up and go to Him. He has a purpose and a plan for each of us, a *calling*. No longer are our lives simply about surviving. We have a God-given purpose.

Sometimes I feel just like Bartimaeus, sitting on the outside, unable to see where I should go, calling out to Jesus to help me. So many other people are around me clamoring to see Jesus as well. They may look more important than me, and they may tell me to calm down. Jesus is busy. I have to remember that Jesus hears me too. He can help me, and He has a direction for me to go.

He has given us everything we need to go that direction and fulfill His purpose for us. Paul points this out in 2 Timothy 3:16-17 when he says, "All Scripture is God-breathed and is useful for teaching, rebuking, correcting, and training in righteousness, so that the servant of God may be thoroughly equipped for every good work." We have God-breathed directions to all that He has given us to do. We are equipped to do all He sets before us! What more could we need?

For some of us, these directions may give the responsibility of taking care of our home and family in the way He's called us. For some, they may result in taking a job outside the home. And for others, it may mean taking up a cause bigger than ourselves or serving those around us. This purpose is different for each of us, as He has made all of us different. Additionally, as we go through life, this purpose may change because *we* change. We grow and mature both spiritually and physically. He may also have different purposes for us when we are in different places.

My challenge for all of us is to find what God has called us to do *today*. Doing what He called us to do each day will lead to fulfilling what He called us to do for a lifetime.

Finding my calling took some life experience and a lot of time. Like many of us, I tried just about everything. I volunteered for anything, especially if it meant organizing things. But whether it involved a gift I had or not, I would take on anything and everything because I felt it was my responsibility. We've all felt that way at times. "If I don't do it, no one else will."

I have since learned to first seek God's face in all things, this area included. I needed His direction as I searched for the gifts and abilities He had given me. It was a process. I believe trying many different things is sometimes a good idea as we often learn more about ourselves and in the process discover abilities we did not know we had. My challenge was the fact that I did not seek God's guidance and do what He asked me to do. Frequently, guilt would drive me more than anything else. I have come to understand that God has a place and a purpose for everyone, and I cannot do everything.

Once I understood more about the gifts God had given me, I found that I still didn't need to jump into every opportunity that could use my gifts. I had to step back and learn that not everything was my duty. I then learned to seek God as I sought out ways to serve.

As I worked through this aspect, God brought me my husband. Since marrying him, I've stepped back and waited much more patiently on God to guide me to areas of service or ministry. Sometimes this takes bringing my husband along to meetings at church or similar places to hold my hand down. I tend to stick my hand up whenever anyone solicits volunteers. I don't get involved in quite as much these days. But when I do, I've found that what I'm able to offer is better quality, and it's given with a greater sense of purpose.

One caveat to this is the fact we sometimes need to take part in things which are not in our "gift" area because someone needs help. For example, after a program at church, we may just need to help move chairs or pick up trash. Sometimes, we simply need to serve. God calls us to be Jesus in the flesh to those around us. This may very well mean assisting in everyday things. Such opportunities abound—like taking dinner to a sick friend, watching the neighbor's children, writing a word of encouragement to someone, or just helping out in the church nursery. These small things show the tangible love of Jesus to those around us.

God addresses this area of gifts multiple times in the Bible. Romans 12 gives us an interesting perspective, though. "We have different gifts, according to the grace he has given us" (Romans 12:6). He then points out some of the gifts He has given to individuals, which is immediately followed with an awesome description of how to do such things. "Love must be sincere. Hate what is evil; cling to what is good. Be devoted to one another in brotherly love. Honor one another above yourselves. Never be lacking in zeal, but keep your spiritual fervor, serving the Lord. Be joyful in hope, patient in affliction, faithful in prayer" (Romans 12:9-12).

Notice that He starts the explanation with love. I believe this is the foundation of the Christian life. Imagine how successful we would be as Christians if we simply loved as Jesus did, or even if we just loved Jesus for exactly who He is. Our life focus would be about serving Him, regardless of circumstances, or what we're doing, knowing that every single thing we do could have eternal significance. We would really become all He has called us to be.

He has given us all gifts to use in service to Him, but the only way to be truly successful is to fall in love with Him. We must keep that "spiritual fervor," being joyful, patient, and faithful. Trusting in the God who made us, we must daily strive to seek out ways to love and allow Him to use us in whatever He chooses.

In this journey of seeking out our gifts and finding where God would have us to serve, realize that we may not be right in every decision, but some things are worth a try. I had no idea that I possessed some of my gifts until I stepped out on faith and attempted something new.

Through accepting new opportunities, I've also discovered that some gifts are not my calling. A small church I attended needed a Music Director—not a Music Minister, *per se*, as they did not have a choir, but just someone to lead the music during worship services. What a blessing God bestowed on them when I did *not* volunteer! But I did recommend my friend who studied music for a year and a half while attending college. In the bargain I made for volunteering her, I agreed to help by singing in a little praise team.

As a point of reference, I did sing in the church youth choir in high school, but was never given a solo part or asked to sing any kind of "special music" during worship services. I was willing, though, so I helped my friend. Once in this position, she needed individuals who would sing "special music." Suffice it to say, that during my two attempts no one immediately left the building, and they were all gracious as they thanked me for my "willingness." Notice no words synonymous with music or beautiful were used.

Sometimes we just have to be willing to try something to see if that may be where God wants us to serve. And if we find that it is not, we can fulfill our initial commitment and understand that we may have never known had we not been willing to take a risk. We will all make mistakes along the way, but God's desire is for us to continuously strive to love and serve Him with everything. By the way, I have yet to sing a solo anywhere since that time—and there are many who should be very thankful!

As we go through life, we'll find that God's calling on our lives may change as well. Until I had children, the idea of not working outside the home had never occurred to me. Rocket science, I know. Nevertheless, our journey takes us through different stages in life, circumstances that change us, experiences that deepen our spiritual walk, and it may even follow curves that take us in a different direction. We may find ourselves down the road in a much different place than we had pictured, but God had it planned all along.

Our responsibility is to be obedient to Him. Obedience means following His call today, and then getting up tomorrow and doing it again, moment by moment seeking out where He would have us. This can also be exciting as we move from place to place, which we do periodically in the military. He may have a completely different plan for us at the new duty station than He did at the last. We simply need to have a heart that is willing to do whatever and go wherever He calls us. This military life becomes an adventure—and an awesome one at that. Think of all the possibilities—the opportunities. It could be amazing to see where we will be in ten or fifteen years as we daily walk with the God who leads us.

God has given us all talents and abilities that we can use for His glory. It's what God designed us to do. Whether this means being a stay-at-home mom or taking on the cause of the more helpless around the world, our individual calling is still a calling from God. None is more important than the other. Just to think that the God of the universe designed us specifically with certain gifts and abilities, and loved us enough to carve out a plan just for our lives is very exciting.

Most of us would dearly love a letter from God, complete with a detailed road map for our lives, but that's not how it works. He asks us to trust Him on faith and to seek Him daily. This is how the relationship grows—one step of faith at a time. If we knew the whole plan ahead of time, we might not check in with Him daily. Checking in frequently is the key.

As cheerleaders encounter new stunts, they may be a little leery in the beginning. However, they've all been taught to give everything they have in their performance of the stunt because if they hesitate they could get hurt or even hurt someone else. They have to go at it with everything they have, using all their muscles, coordination, and training acquired over years of practice. In the end, they accomplish awesome things. As we seek to do what God called us to do, we may be asked to do some things that make us hesitate. Just like the cheerleaders, we have to be willing to go into the stunt with everything we have so that we too can accomplish amazing things!

Cannonball Moments

Much like a cheerleader, our first inclination might be to just try a little at first and not go in wholeheartedly. But we shouldn't! We should catapult in heart, mind, and strength.

Have you ever been to the local swimming pool in the summer and watched in amazement the people who hesitantly test the water? First a toe. Barely a ripple. They may sit by the edge of the pool dangling their feet, not quite ready to go all the way in. They might, eventually, make it to the steps and wade into the water. Or not. Sometimes they never make it off the edge because the water is too cold or they worry their hair might get wet.

Then there are those who immediately strip to their swimsuit, back up as far as they can (without getting in trouble from the lifeguard), and dash to the pool. Catapulting themselves from the side, they perform a perfect cannonball and end up completely submerged in the water, drenching everyone within splashing distance. They are now ready to have fun, not wasting one minute "checking the water."

The second group is having a blast, but sadly, the first group may never experience the joy of the water, the awesome feeling of submerging themselves and gliding through the pool. The freedom that feeling can bring is incredible! The first group may never even learn to swim, never learn to love the water because they never tried. My goodness, the things they will miss!

As children of God, we should respond to our calling with faith and a cannonball leap off the edge. Many times we go into life just like the first group. We hesitate, sometimes pretending we're just testing the waters to see if that's where God wants us, but are we really just holding back because we fear that failure may be on the horizon? What God wants in us is a cannonball-moment-life. A life completely sold out to Him where we jump in with everything we have whether the water is cold or not, trusting the One who called us. In this experience we learn to swim and the joy is incomparable!

We may jump into something and instead of enjoying a cannonball moment, it may feel more like a belly flop—just like my singing experience! Singing might not be my calling, but I learned in the process, and I'm glad I tried. By the way, I still love to sing. I have just found that I do better with songs that include motions so I can distract those around me who have to listen.

When you're longing to find a place to serve, and you're seeking God's direction, just jump in. Don't stand back, give just a little, or test it out with your pinky toe—jump in. It's a difficult thing to do at times, but so worth it in the end. God wants all of us. And even if we make mistakes, His desire is for our heart to be sold out to Him.

King David made many mistakes, from his relationship with Bathsheba, to losing control of the throne to his son. Yet Samuel said, "The Lord has sought out a man after his own heart and anointed him leader of his people" (1 Samuel 13:14).

God knew everything David would do and yet He called David "a man after his own heart." God was not fooled into thinking that David was perfect, but He did understand that even in his most sinful times, David's desire always came back to pleasing his Lord. He sincerely desired to accomplish what the Lord wanted. When he failed, he was truly brokenhearted and returned to the comfort and grace of his loving, heavenly Father. His heart was in the right place. Failing was not the issue. The point was that David continued to strive toward the goal. He kept working at it.

David passed on this lesson to his son in 1 Chronicles 28:9. He told him, "And you, my son Solomon, acknowledge the God of your father, and serve him with wholehearted devotion and with a willing mind, for the Lord searches every heart and understands every motive behind the thoughts." David completely understood God's desire. He knew God looked past all of the mess-ups and saw David's heart. He wanted his son to understand that his actions were important, but his "wholehearted devotion" was vital. May we follow David's advice. Desiring to serve wholly and completely, knowing we'll mess up, but striving to always be what God wants us to be nonetheless. Having a heart for service to our God—this is our desire.

This reminds me again of Bartimaeus. He shouted to Jesus for help. When Jesus called him, Bartimaeus got up, threw off his coat, and went to Him. He was serious about talking to Jesus and ready for whatever was asked of him. Bartimaeus may have heard stories of Jesus putting mud on men's eyes to heal their blindness, or being asked to go for a swim to cure their leprosy. He didn't know what Jesus was going to ask, but he was ready anyway.

I pray that we do the same. That we shout out to Jesus for help, and when we hear His voice that we jump up, throw of the junk we carry around, and run to Him. We must be ready for any assignment He may have for us and have a heart wholly devoted in service to Him.

This was the first time that Bartimaeus met Jesus. When he got to Jesus, he was asked, "What do you want me to do for you?" (Mark 10:51) Bartimaeus asked Jesus to heal him, and then it says, "Immediately he received his sight and followed Jesus along the road" (Mark 10:52). This is where we all start. Simply asking for Jesus' help and then following Him.

From this point we practice this same scenario over and over. We shout out to Jesus. He answers and then we follow. This provides the training and practice needed to eagerly follow Him, and wholeheartedly devote our lives in service to Him. As our faith and relationship with the Father grow, He will ask more of us because we understand and trust more.

These challenges help us become stronger because we've seen Jesus work around us. Think of the cheerleaders who train and practice their stunts. They, too, start out simply learning to jump correctly, moving then to cartwheels and round-offs, adding in some flips, and then learning to do group stunts. Like these cheerleaders, we practice with the little things until God engages us in the great things.

Cheerleaders are athletes in the true sense of the word. They practice and train constantly. They attempt things that might make them hesitate, but they jump in anyway because they know they must give their all or someone, including themselves, might get hurt. They give everything they have physically and mentally to accomplish phenomenal stunts—and smile the entire time.

Military wives give everything we have to truly answer the call God has placed on our lives—hopefully with a smile. That call reaches far beyond being a military wife. He has a specific calling for each of us and asks simply that we jump in. Many of us have accomplished awesome things from the legacy we've left with our children to changing the lives of those God has brought into our paths. If we daily seek God's will, years from now we'll reflect on the awesome stunts we've performed in a lifetime, simply by taking little steps every day. As we perform such stunts, we'll get tired and sore from the exertion. We will no doubt encounter days when we'd rather take a break and maybe have a seat in the bleachers for a bit. As cheerleaders, days will come when the weather doesn't cooperate and the scoreboard doesn't look so good. Challenges we will encounter along this journey. How do we deal with such things? What is our attitude when days are harder to bear and everything seems like an uphill battle? We all have those days when lying down and giving up seems like a good option. But when times are toughest, we military wives say, "Bring it on!"

Chapter Three

Bring It On!

In every game I've ever witnessed, cheerleaders have stayed on the field with the team, regardless of the weather. With snow blowing sideways, sleet coming down, or one hundred degree temperatures, the game goes on . . . and last I checked, so did the cheerleaders. You'll see them wearing layers and layers of clothing, and at times huddled together, but never sitting inside watching the game on a screen. They signed up for this, and by golly, they will fulfill their commitment. They will be there until the final quarter ends, and then still hang out to celebrate or console, whichever the case may be.

Personally, I feel for them. I've had jobs that required me to brave the weather—from hiking through sleet to saddling horses in pouring rain. Those days of working in the sleet, snow, and rain were *not* my favorite. I would have much preferred to stay snuggled in bed, but something about receiving a paycheck motivates me to get moving. Weird, I know.

These cheerleaders, though, especially in high school, did not receive a paycheck. In fact, most of them probably paid to participate. Some might think the cheerleader's motivation was just to be out in front of the crowd and look good, but I haven't seen many people who look particularly attractive while freezing in the sleet. No, this was dedication.

As young cheerleaders they might not have understood the challenges associated with the position. We all remember being sixteen or seventeen years old. Chances are these young cheerleaders didn't really think very far ahead about anything. Cheerleading was just a great idea. Their parents may have tried to warn them about cold and miserable games, but they were probably convinced and determined that cheerleading was what they wanted, nonetheless.

I don't know if older cheerleaders, those at college or professional levels, plan for bad weather. Maybe they assume a blizzard won't happen on game day—that it will hold off until they can be cozy and warm inside.

I wouldn't have thought any differently. I mean, really . . . who actually plans on standing out in a blizzard? Football only runs August though January. Surely the weather won't be *too* bad. Regardless, they took the job—and all the fun that goes with it. No amount of cute bows and glittery eye shadow will warm a body during a blizzard. Now performing the job—cheering and stunts—could quite possibly warm them up.

We, as military wives, signed up for this too! This military-wife job was voluntary. Either we married guys who were already in the military, or the decision was made after we were married to join. Either way we said "I do" and our husbands signed the dotted line, regardless of the order in which it was done. So here we are!

We can relate to the young cheerleader who had no idea what was involved in this escapade. The military is an institution full of traditions and pride, not to mention military balls where we're able to dress in formal attire. In theory, we're able to enjoy prom repeatedly—which is great for those of us who never went to prom in high school! The ceremony and reputation alone can get a girl excited about the upcoming prospects of military life—and then add in the fact that our husbands look good all gussied up! We would marry them all over again every time they put on their dress uniform.

Then, smack! Military life sets in. They wear their utility uniform with the fancy cargo pockets and dusted off boots every day. They even set the alarm for 5:00a.m., or some other crazy hour. Who knew real people get up at such a time—to exercise of all things! Oh yes, and then there is the moving. I do not mind visiting different places, but setting up a house and taking down a house is for the birds! Then the whopper—deployment, again. These exciting experiences do not include the "normal" things of life, like the three-hour wait in the emergency room for one of the kids, the car breaking down when our husbands are in the field, and making ends meet now that we are rich.

Guess what! We just met the blizzard! Sometimes we'll even have days when we feel like the sleet came first, then snow, and then additional sleet to make it nice and slick on the snow's surface. We may even have days we'd like to call the game early and head inside . . . we really don't know much about football anyway, so how can we really be of any help? Amazingly enough, I've never seen a football game called early for weather-related reasons—or any other reason. They always finished the game.

Attitude

One attribute cheerleaders and military wives undoubtedly have in common is attitude. Watching the cheerleaders come out with a spring in their step and their chins held high, they are the epitome of attitude. This is not a condemnation by any means. Attitude is a requirement. They are about to take part in a competition that has everything to do with their school pride. Their full intention is to walk off the field as part of a victorious team. Confidence in the outcome and persistence in the battle, this is the only way to win.

I have learned in life that many things are all about perspective and attitude. Our success is highly dependent upon how we tackle the objective. If we start off with even an inkling of an idea that we might fail, we've left the door open to failure. We must stand tall, arms crossed, feet wide, mind set, and determined that victory will be our end result. This is a visual of Paul's words to the Corinthians when he said "Therefore, my dear brothers, stand firm. Let nothing move you. Always give yourselves fully to the work of the Lord, because you know that your labor in the Lord is not in vain" (1 Corinthians 15:58).

Just recently, I watched attitude in action. My sister teaches some intense and challenging group fitness classes. Many of her students are in their twenties, but some are a little further along like me.

Keeping this in mind, I visited her classes and enjoyed the workouts, although I have none of my sister's skill and grace. The classes required persistence, a small amount of coordination, lots of sweat, and some attitude. Interestingly enough, we were expected to perform many of the skills and exercises with a certain flair. If not done properly, one might very well look silly. Performing the moves with attitude wasn't required because it looked good. Showing attitude meant the participants were putting their heart and minds to the task at hand instead of just going through the motions. They get a much better workout this way, and in turn, they are more successful in accomplishing their goal of physical fitness.

Cheerleading, and consequently, military-wife life are much like this. We can go through the motions and fulfill the expectations, but to truly be successful requires attitude. We must engage our hearts and our minds in the task at hand. Whatever comes, we must take it head on with attitude and confidence knowing we are not in this alone. We are reminded of this very fact in Hebrews.

> Therefore, brothers, since we have confidence to enter the Most Holy Place by the blood of Jesus, by a new and living way opened for us through the curtain, that is, his body, and since we have a great priest over the house of God, let us draw near to God with a sincere heart in full assurance of faith, having our hearts sprinkled to cleanse us from a guilty conscience and having our bodies washed with pure water. Let us hold unswervingly

to the hope we profess, for he who promised is faithful.
(Hebrews 10:19-23)

This is attitude at its best. We can go straight to the Father, the God of the universe, for any and every thing because Jesus made the way. Believing in the promises He made, we hold to the faith we profess—we live what we believe. This gives us the confidence to know we serve the God of all creation, and He can handle anything! Focus, determination, attitude. When my mind is focused and Jesus is leading me, I can tackle anything, so—BRING IT ON! With Him by my side, who—or what—am I to fear?

Challenges

I am in this for the long haul. My husband is stuck with me until I go to meet Jesus. Our intent is to make the best of this life. Lord willing, we will be faithful to Him and to each other for the duration.

Jesus is my strength and my shield—from the freezing rain or driving wind. David said it perfectly when he said, "The Lord is my strength and my shield; my heart trusts in him, and I am helped" (Psalm 28:7). His protection is all I have, but it is all I need. I cannot imagine this life without Him. Nor could I imagine life without the man He gave me. Only God knows the number of our days. I plan to do my very best to be the wife I am called to be and let God take care of the rest—including the man I love so much.

We will all encounter challenges. If we have not met them yet, we better dig our heels in and get ready, some days will be doozies. These challenges come in the form of actual physical separation from our spouses, struggles with trust and love in our marriages, personal aches and pains—whether physical or emotional, relationship issues with our personal or military families, and in many other ways. More than likely we will experience more than one, if not all, of these challenges in our time with the military.

My suggestion is to get on our knees with the God of the universe, give it to Him, and then stand up with a whole new attitude—BRING

IT ON! Whatever life may throw at us, whatever we may encounter, God and only God can bring us through whole and complete. He can take care of issues we have no idea how to handle, mend relationships we had decided to abandon due to failure, hold us and our husbands together when there are thousands of miles between us, and be our peace when everything else in the world has gone completely haywire. *He* is the answer to everything. We must also remember Paul's encouragement in Philippians 4:13 when he said, "I can do everything through him who gives me strength." If Paul can do it, so can we!

Some days we will struggle to put one foot in front of the other. We'll want to hibernate for a while or maybe quit altogether. Just hang on! David gives us some direction and encouragement in these times through Psalm 55:22 when he said, "Cast your cares on the Lord and he will sustain you; he will never let the righteous fall." How awesome is it to give our burdens to the Lord and then rest in the fact that He loves us and has enough power to take care of it all?

The day will come when rejoicing abounds. We will stand on the field with the sun shining, a cool breeze blowing, and victory on the scoreboard! On this day we will look to the heavens and say "thank you" to the God who brought us through.

This day may not come as early as we expect—it never seems to. It may not come in the form we thought it would, but no matter how or when this exciting moment comes, we will feel the joy in our hearts and be able to look back and see God's hand in all of the circumstances along the way. In fact, we will most probably experience this day over and over as God delivers, provides, protects, and sustains us for a lifetime.

So for today—let's start on our knees, let Him fill us up, and then take the day. "Be joyful always; pray continually; give thanks in all circumstances, for this is God's will for you in Christ Jesus" (1 Thessalonians 5:16-18). Paul lays it out quite plainly, showing us that we must be joyful, continue to pray, and be thankful. Joy is a little challenging on some days as we all know, but we must not get confused between joy and happiness. Happiness is wholly dependent on attitude and circumstances. Joy, on the other hand, is dependent upon our foundation of faith. We have to rest in the fact God is in control and He loves us more than anything in the universe. We understand joy in those moments when everything seems to be an uphill battle and God still fills us with His peace and hope. Now that is cool!

Christ also encourages us to live today without worry for tomorrow. He says, "Therefore do not worry about tomorrow, for tomorrow will worry about itself. Each day has enough trouble of its own" (Matthew 6:34). We all know at times we can be our own worst enemy. We can allow circumstances to overwhelm us as we deal with the things of today and begin to fret over what we will deal with tomorrow. Jesus so wants us to rest in our faith, trusting His word, and allowing Him to take our burdens. Each day will surely come on its own, but take this day and make it exactly what God intended it to be—a day of victory, hope, and peace for us.

Growth

We may have been like the young cheerleader and not had any idea what the future held. This might have actually been to our advantage. In this instance, we had no time to be anxious about what might be down the road, because we didn't know what to expect. We trusted and believed the best was yet to come, and we were right.

On the other hand, some of us might have been experienced in military life and accepted this challenge knowing full well what would be asked of us. We walked into this military-wife life knowing exactly what lay ahead and we were willing to take it on. We had thought through the bad weather days, the days we would lose a game, the days when players might be injured. We knew about all of it, and yet we voluntarily accepted the challenge because we knew this was where we were supposed to be. Ideally, while walking into this challenge with somewhat complete knowledge of the struggles ahead, we have not let the understanding of what *might* happen hinder us from enjoying the exciting things that *do* happen.

Whether we're like the young cheerleader or the experienced one, we have an awesome opportunity to grow and learn, and see all that God can do in us. We have the chance to take on challenges with excitement, and enjoy the experience of allowing God to take control of it all. So dare we say—BRING IT ON! Whatever this life has for me, I am ready to tackle and conquer. I am not a fan of foul weather, but I'm willing to prove I can hang in there because my God is leading me, and with Him I can claim victory—even before the game begins.

Now how do we accomplish such things? It's not an easy task. It's no walk in the park. Know that achieving this confidence, and in turn true victory, is work and it takes some time. Just like cheerleaders, we'll have to put in some training and practice. Most people don't like to practice, me included. It's not nearly as exciting as the game itself, but it is necessary, nonetheless.

Before we do anything else, we must devote ourselves to a regular, focused *prayer* life. This is our most prized skill, and mastering it will work wonders . . . literally. Having a focused conversation with God on a regular basis and learning to live our lives in a state of prayer is the bottom line. Knowing that God is constantly with us, we can reach out to Him at any time, including when we're washing dishes or driving the car. He becomes our constant companion. How awesome is that?

Paul emphasizes this point to the church at Ephesus when he tells them to "pray in the Spirit on all occasions with all kinds of prayers and requests" (Ephesians 6:18). He doesn't tell them to pray when they are scared, lonely, or challenged. He tells them to pray on all occasions, even on days when we don't think we have anything to say. These instructions also encourage us to bring all of our prayers and requests to God, even the ones that seem so miniscule at the time. God knows anyway, we might as well tell Him.

Prayer gives us the opportunity to develop a relationship with our God. Just like with our other relationships, communication is of utmost importance. If we fail to talk to each other, we fail to know each other. Communication works this way with God too. One of the most challenging aspects of this conversation for me is that we not only need to *talk* to God, we also need to *listen*. In my own pray life, it's easy for me to get so caught up in telling God everything I think He needs to know, I fail to hear what He has to say. Focused prayer time can also provide a great opportunity to see what God is doing in our lives. If we write down our petitions and the lessons God is teaching us, we can periodically check back and see not only how God has answered prayers, but how much we've grown in our faith. Keeping a journal with these notes provides a very tangible way to see God work.

In addition to spending time in prayer, we must spend time *reading His Word*. Setting time aside to study the Bible is definitely worthwhile. It's a wonderful way for us to see how God has worked throughout history, and it allows Him to speak to us through the written word.

If we do not have a specific Bible study to work from, we can start anywhere and read. Many people start with the book of John in the New Testament, as the message is simple and the book is easier than some to understand. Other books I enjoy are Hebrews, Philippians, Psalms, and Ruth. Additionally, I have found it very helpful to have a commentary or similar such book available to clarify some areas I may not completely understand. This is not mandatory, though. The expectation is to read His Word.

Prior to even opening His Word, if we ask God to show us what He'd like us to learn, we'll be amazed at how valuable this time will become. Sometimes we lose sight of the fact that our Bible is a living letter to us, providing direction from a holy God. Paul, reminding Timothy of the Scripture's purpose said, "All Scripture is God-breathed and is useful for teaching, rebuking, correcting, and training in righteousness, so that the man of God may be thoroughly equipped for every good work" (2 Timothy 3:16-17).

The purpose of these Scriptures is to prepare and train us to accomplish all God has planned for us to do. The Bible operates as a guidebook, and it provides insight into the lives of others who have gone before us. Spending time in God's Word opens our eyes to see miracle after miracle and the intimate relationship God has with His people. We are also reminded He is the same yesterday, today, and forever. This means He is as involved in my life as He was in David's, Moses', or Paul's lives. What a blessing to know He is just as intimately involved with me as He was in the lives of those we consider patriarchs of our faith.

Spending time reading Scripture is quite possibly one of our most challenging aspects in growth, and yet it is so very vital to a healthy and mature Christian faith. God took the time to write down exactly what He wanted to say, nothing more and nothing less, to give us everything we need to live this life exactly the way He wants us to. Why would we not want to take time to read such instructions? I'm guilty of this as much as anyone. I read so many other things and spend my time doing things I deem important, and yet reading my Bible should be ranked at the very top of my list of important things to do. My prayer is that we all make this a top priority so we "may be thoroughly equipped for every good work" (2 Timothy 3:17).

In addition to prayer and Bible study time, we need *regular fellowship* with other believers. We need to find a church home wherever we are. We will never find a perfect church because they are filled with imperfect people. As a Christian, though, God has a place He has prepared for each of us to worship, fellowship, and serve. We need to find this place and become involved. We need to participate in worship, join a small group Bible study (formerly called Sunday school), and find a place of service.

Attending church on a regular basis can be a struggle, especially when we are on our own (i.e., husbands are deployed) or we have children. Getting everyone clothed, fed, and out the door can present a battle we have no desire to fight. Hebrews gives us guidance and hope in this area. "Hold unswervingly to the hope we profess, for he who promised is faithful. And let us consider how we may spur one another on toward love and good deeds. Let us not give up meeting together, as some are in the habit of doing, but let us encourage one another – and all the more as you see the Day approaching" (Hebrews 10:23-25).

Being in God's house, interacting with His people, and worshipping Him on a regular basis will make a gigantic difference in our spiritual lives, as well as our family lives. Making it a regular habit can change the expectation of all family members and quite possibly make it an activity everyone looks forward to. This time with others provides encouragement, as well as accountability, strengthening our spiritual walk even more.

Finding a church home as we move from one place to another can be a difficult process. Finding a new home can many times be easier than finding a new church. Deciding which churches to visit, dropping kids off by themselves in classes, finding a place where beliefs match ours—and where God is moving—can be difficult, yet the rewards are amazing. Our family has found that God chooses a place for us long before we arrive, but finding it sometimes takes a few tries. The search becomes almost like a treasure hunt, but the treasure we find in the churches we make home is awesome.

All three aspects of our Christian walk—prayer, Bible study, and worship are important, and the rewards for time spent on such things are the peace which passes all understanding and a maturity we never thought obtainable. If we make spending time with the Father and other believers a priority, the results will be astounding! Let's not give up.

Stick Together

Now before we call this pep rally to a close, take one more look at those cheerleaders on the field during those crazy winter storms, huddled together for warmth and protection from the elements. They stick together to help and encourage each other during the challenging times. How cold (and very alone) would they be if they had to stand out in the blizzard by themselves?

Sticking together is not a bad idea. Wherever we're planted, God provides others to help and encourage us, and asks us to do the same for them. In the military, these people are called our battle buddies. We find these buddies in military spouse organizations, our local churches, women's Bible study groups on or off post, or all of the above. In today's world, these battle buddies can even include online forums, social networking sites, and blogs. We need to stick together.

Most of our buddies will be with us for a time. Ideally, these are godly women who help us see what God is doing and call us out when we're straying off the path. Honesty is a wonderful thing; and when it is done in love, it becomes even better. If these ladies are military wives, this can be a great advantage. Much as we have in common with the rest of the world, we are still sometimes in our own unique community.

All of these battle buddies will impact our lives, but along the way, we'll find those few who are our battle buddies for duration—those trusted friends who will last a lifetime. These women are God's gift to us as we learn from them, are encouraged by them, and give back to them. These confidantes are few and far between. Cherish them, because even with miles between us, we will still be connected. They are truly a blessing.

Notice in every instance we used the term "women." We must always guard our marriages. Having a male individual become such an intimate part of our lives can open a door we didn't plan to open. We will share our hearts with these women, as well as, quite a bit of time. If we do not choose wisely, we will find ourselves very vulnerable to Satan's schemes. We must guard our hearts and our marriages—for all we are worth. Having women fill these roles of friend, confidante, and encourager is of primary importance.

God brings these special people to us to help us weather the storms. He also allows us to help them in return. What a wonderful opportunity He has given us. This is our chance to be His tangible ear to listen, hand to hold, and arms to hug. We must love people as God has called us to, huddling together when the sleet and blizzards come, fanning each other when the temperatures rise, and throwing parties during good times. Hang on to those special battle buddies; they may be God's gift for a season, or even for a lifetime.

This life can be adventurous and challenging—an exciting journey that just may surprise us along the way. Expect it. We must determine today that we're in this for the long haul—rain, sleet, snow, or one hundred degree temperatures. Remember, this was a voluntary position—and we signed up for it.

God will bless and sustain us as we stick to the covenant made with our husbands and our God on the day we said "I do." In this relationship, we have to learn to give and to receive, remembering it is God we serve and not man. We do this to the very best of our ability because we made a promise.

Finding those battle buddies is also vital; God has given us a definite gift in those we call friends. These ladies hold our hands in challenging times, and they rejoice with us during exciting experiences. We must reach out and develop these relationships. Granted, in so doing, we open ourselves up to the possibility of pain in the process, but also to the possibility of wonderful joy.

Above all else, we must make sure our walk with God is where it needs to be. This is quite possibly the most difficult aspect, and yet everything is wholly dependent upon this detail. Prayer, Bible study, and Christian fellowship are essential components to our success in this venture. These are the foundations for the strength and perseverance we will need to possess.

So . . . ready, OKAY! Bring on the storms, bring on the cold, and bring on the heat; know it is coming. Know who our God is and what He can do, and know we are not in this alone. Whatever this military-wife life may have to offer—BRING IT ON!

That's right—BRING IT ON! Through these challenging times, we will find in ourselves gifts and abilities we had no idea we possessed. We will see God at work in our lives and learn to trust Him, regardless of circumstances. This will come in handy when we are faced with inevitable overtime. In military life, few things seem to operate on my schedule, and sometimes they don't even operate exactly on the military's schedule (surprise!). But rest assured, all things happen on God's schedule. Regardless of how the schedule works, we must be prepared for certain change, but how?

Chapter Four

Overtime

The cheerleaders have been at the field for hours. They arrive before the game begins to prepare and warm up. They welcome their team onto the field, and then cheer them on as minutes tick away on the scoreboard. Half-time passes; the cheerleaders continue as energetic and excited as they started. As observers and not participants, most cheerleaders know everything there is to know about cheerleading, but not nearly as much about the games they attend. They study their art to be the best that they can be, but most of the time have little experience or interest in learning or playing football.

One thing every cheerleader understands, though, is that the scoreboard is filled with vital information. Not only does it share statistics like first downs and points scored, it also displays the all-important information of time left in the game. Each cheerleader knows that when time runs out for the fourth quarter, the game is over. It's time to go home. Win or lose, the end of the game signals a time to rest and come back for another day. Planning for this moment, they see it coming and continue giving everything they have, expecting a rest period when time runs out. Whether performing in sunshine or snow, cheerleading can be exhausting. Their muscles get sore and fatigued;

their voices start to go. By the end of the game, they have given all they have to "the cause."

Then the final play arrives; the score is tied. Making one last all-or-nothing play, the team reaches for the end zone one more time. The whistle blows for the game to be over. Everyone holds their breath as players climb off of each other, waiting to view where the ball landed that last time. As anxiety crescendos, they discover that the ball is just inches shy of reaching the objective. A silence hovers over the field as everyone waits to hear the referee say that one word that can cause nervousness and frustration, but can also give hope and expectation. The referee calls OVERTIME!

Everyone in the stands and on the field, including the cheerleaders, believed their team was going to pull it out. That last touchdown was going to take them home. And yet, more minutes are added to the scoreboard. They might be at the field for another thirty minutes or an hour, nobody knows.

Whether planned or not, the cheerleaders stay. They signed up to cheer for this team from the time they run onto the field until the very, very last whistle blows. Exhausted, sore, and hoarse, they continue to cheer. Never done half-heartedly, not one cheerleader finds a bench to sit and rest, or even exits the field to use the restroom. This is their team, their commitment. Regardless of whether or not they were consulted about overtime, they made other plans following the game, or they are completely worn out, these girls hang on until the very end. Believing that their team will finish victoriously, cheerleaders continue to cheer with all the energy they have left.

This dedication goes far beyond wearing a cute little outfit or hoping some guy will notice them. By this time, they have bought into the game, becoming a part of the team. Passing from mere observers to full participants, they have found themselves actively involved in a bigger plan. Though completely exhausted, these cheerleaders have given their hearts, become sold-out supporters, and die-hard believers. Trusting that this whistle would be their last, they had given everything they thought they had to give. Yet, these cheerleaders continue on, whether due to adrenaline or sheer determination, going into overtime with the same enthusiasm and spirit exhibited at the game's start. They are in this for the long haul.

All of this sounds very noble, I know. In looking at cheerleaders through this lens, we come to respect their commitment, their loyalty, and their physical stamina. While sitting in the stands, we follow their lead and cheer as well to the very end. We don't leave the bleachers and many times we don't even sit down. We focus, we cheer, we believe, because the cheerleaders have inspired us to do just that. Their belief and enthusiasm in the cause is contagious.

Military Overtime

Up to this point, the cheerleaders have given what they thought was all they had to the game. They would have believed that nothing was left. At the end of the game, they would have been mentally and physically finished. And yet, as the referees announce overtime, the cheerleaders find within themselves a willingness to give just a little bit more for a little bit longer. They are inspired by the players as they continue to fight for the cause, and they stand on their commitment to hang on until the very end. These ladies have a loyalty to this team and a commitment to fulfill. And regardless of their personal feelings, they stay true to the promise they made.

Have we ever felt this way? As military wives, we experience this same kind of challenge intermittently throughout our husbands' careers, and even sometimes as our husbands' careers draw to a close. When we have given everything we think is possible to give, we're asked to give a little bit more, to hang on a little bit longer. When we feel both mentally and physically exhausted, when we believe we have nothing left to give, our faith, commitment, and sheer determination are the only things helping us to hold on. No doubt, we all have been in this same place at some point in time.

Overtime involves those moments in our lives when we feel that we can't handle our children for one more minute and then get the phone call from our husbands that they will be home later than planned; the times when our husbands are sent to the field and expected home by Thursday, but due to some transportation issue they will not arrive till Saturday. Overtime may even be those times when we wait with great expectation for our husbands to arrive home from a year-long deployment in July, and get the notification that it will now be at least August, maybe even September before they arrive.

Possibly even more challenging than these situations is what can happen when we're planning to leave this military life. This may be due to our husbands' commitments being fulfilled, or they may have reached retirement. Either way, we and our husbands have planned for this day. We may have bought our retirement home, planned to launch a new business, or even started looking at a new career. We've made plans. Our families are ready for the change.

Our minds have adjusted to this new way of thinking. Then in a matter of days or weeks, whether we were ready or not, the initial commitment got extended or the retirement got delayed. Sometimes such things happen involuntarily, and sometimes they're caused by our own decisions, but either way, it's still considered overtime.

Run!

The challenge of overtime affects all of us at one time or another. We struggle with the changes, and attempt not to pass out from exhaustion and fatigue. We try to adjust our mindset to accept and be successful in the new course. If anyone is like me, this can be quite overwhelming. I work well with schedules. I do great when someone lays out the agenda and we follow the plan, or when I know exactly what is expected and for how long. The uphill battle for me comes with the overtime. Everything one might consider a schedule, agenda, or plan has now been thrown out the window.

My adjustment to overtime works very much like my running history. When I go out for a run, I do much better when I know where the end is. I am much more successful when I can see the big picture and understand completely what is expected of me. I love to have the plan mapped out in advance. If I can actually have a topographically correct to-scale-map, that is even better, knowing where the start and finish lines are and what is expected in between. Additionally, I like to know who is running with me, and really appreciate it when they show up on time. These runs are my most successful. I get my mind set on the objective at hand, and can hang on for the duration if I know how long I have to hang on. Makes perfect sense, right?

I've been on runs with groups that are slightly different than this, though. Group training runs are not my favorite. Usually the group consists of an instructor and a small group of individuals who are approximately at the same ability level. We all take off, and the instructor is the only one who knows the path and the destination. We just run, at the pace they set for however long they decide to go.

These are not runs I consider fun. During these runs, we sometimes pass the same place more than once, and still we keep going. The thought crosses my mind that we should finish soon; we must have gone at least ten miles or so. The worst, though, is when we pass the place we were expecting to stop. As we come to that place, our hearts race, knowing, for sure, that this is it. Thank goodness! We were about to die. Then, to our amazement, we keep on running!

When this happens, I can feel everything in me deflate. I thought I was strong enough, that I could hold on, and now I am not so sure. At these moments, everything in me begins to hurt, with all of my heart I want to quit, and my attitude takes a definite nose-dive. How long will this go on? Can I be pushed any further? This last question is where I begin to understand the purpose of this torture, because sometimes that's exactly what it feels like—torture.

I'm tired and exhausted at this point, wanting more than anything to stop and walk. Why do I have to keep going? What is the good in that? I've learned, when I am pushed beyond what I thought I could do, I become stronger, both mentally and physically. James, probably Jesus' brother, understood this aspect when he wrote the book named after him. He explains, "Consider it pure joy, my brothers, whenever you face trials of many kinds, because you know that the testing of your faith develops perseverance. Perseverance must finish its work so that you may be mature and complete, not lacking anything" (James 1:2-4).

This is a process. He starts with trials, moves to faith, and finishes with perseverance. He knows, just like we do, trials will come. They'll test the faith that is already in place, resulting in perseverance. Faith must be our primary objective. We have to remember, regardless of how we see things, God is still in control and He loves us. This faith is defined in Hebrews 11:1 when it says, "Now faith is being sure of what we hope for and certain of what we do not see."

God does not have levels of faith, just one. He simply expects us to trust Him, and in turn, experience great and awesome things. In Matthew 27:20, Jesus explained to His disciples that even if they had "faith as small as a mustard seed" they could say to a mountain, "Move from here to there and it will move. Nothing will be impossible for you." Jesus wanted them to understand that if they had any faith at all, they could do amazing things.

The Instructor

We, too, can move mountains. With this foundation of faith, we can take on trials. To be successful in this run, we have to keep going, trusting that the instructor knows our abilities and will challenge us accordingly. This instructor we follow is none other than the God we serve. God sets the pace, determines the distance, and chooses the route and destination. He also decides who forms each group.

That's correct—God planned for us to be joined up with our husbands to form our ability groups. In reality, my husband can run much faster and probably much farther than I, but in God's estimation we match up perfectly. He has set a course for us to follow together, and He hangs with us through the entire distance.

Our job is to stay with the group and finish. We must stay committed to the covenant we made and keep on going, regardless of how much our knees hurt or how much air we think our lungs can take in. God knows what we can handle. He knows where we've been, and He knows where we're headed. He has a route already mapped out. Just hang with the cadence, focus on what is ahead, and keep running.

In this light, we come to understand God's hand on all we encounter. We learn to see that God determines our paths, not our husbands. Many times in these overtime experiences, we start to think our husbands have complete control over all of the circumstances. In reality, the only one who has complete control is the God of it all. As a couple, we must stay with the pace and keep on trucking until God says we're finished.

This is many times easier said than done. Times will come when we want to drop out of the run or lag behind. Our legs get tired, our lungs feel like they are going to explode, our knees hurt, or we just get bored because the scenery seems to stay the same. Staying focused and committed, we must continue to stick with the guy next to us and follow the instructor's directions, keeping pace with the cadence God calls in our lives. The excitement will come when we finish, when we see where we've been and how far we've come. How thankful we'll be for the strength the run has given us, for the little push every now and then from the instructor, and for the partner He provided . . . because, amazingly enough, we really do run together perfectly.

I've lagged behind on some runs, and sometimes I've been pushed farther than I thought I could go. God does the same thing with us. At times in this military life, I feel like I've given everything I have to give and God pushes me some more. He knows I can go farther and be stronger. He knows how much my legs and lungs have left to give—He made them. His desire for me is to be better when I finish than when I start, and pushing me is how I get there.

Overtime gives me a big push—the part of the run where we're already tired and we hit a long uphill stretch. I can do this. We can do this, focusing on the steps in front of us and singing ourselves a little song along the way. Before we know it, we'll be at the top of the hill and headed down the other side, amazed that we made it . . . and thankful for the downhill time.

Don't get me wrong, I still experience many times when I'd like the map in advance. I'd love to know where I start and finish. If I know the distance and destination, I can use the oldest pair of running shoes and run on the hottest day of the year, and still be successful because I know the plan. In dealing with my attitude during this run, I've learned the difference comes in my expectations.

Expectations

Expectations—this is a huge word for me. I am schedule-oriented, goal-driven. I like to have a plan (preferably of my own making) before anything ever starts. This happens when I run, sit in meetings, or even go to church. I love having a bulletin in worship service that actually tells everything that will happen. It's much like an agenda to me; I can check things off as we go. God has spoken to me many times outside of a set agenda, but I sure do like to have it. I have a level of expectation at events, meetings, or whatever I attend. It works well for me since my husband is much the same way.

The challenge comes when those expectations aren't met. We've all sat in meetings where it took two hours to finish something that could have been completed in thirty minutes, but people just kept talking. I'm very thankful no one has ever taken my blood pressure during these times. I really have to work at calming down and simply changing my expectations. This meeting scenario, as well as my running experience, is exactly like overtime—the times when I thought I was finished, and yet was still asked to keep going just a little bit longer.

These overtime moments are difficult for me. I set my mind on the goal or destination and when someone changes that, especially without much explanation, I'm challenged. Whether it's a year-long deployment that turns into fifteen months, or a planned retirement that's now on hold for a few more years, I struggle with moments like these. Our commitment, stamina, and attitude are all tested, and we may even wonder at times if we'll make it to the end.

I talked to a retired Air Force officer's wife who shared with me a story that put many things into perspective and encouraged me in my quest to finish the game victoriously. Her husband retired from the Air Force about twenty-five years before I met them. At the time we were introduced, they were in their mid-eighties.

As the story goes, the husband had planned to retire from the military, so they both decided to start making arrangements for this new adventure in their lives. Part of the plans included the wife working together with another military wife as they prepared to open their own business.

They developed a business plan, chose the building, and purchased a portion of the initial stock. Then, overtime was called. The husband communicated with his wife that the Air Force asked him to stay on a couple more years and offered him a promotion along with a nice duty station to go with it. What did they do?

I'm sure you know the answer. Through a decision they made together, they stayed in for a couple more years and never went back to the business. In talking with her years later, I never even heard a hint of regret or bitterness in her voice. She was willing to make the sacrifice. They were still happily married many years later, and even held hands during their daily morning walks. They were committed to being together, whatever this life might bring.

Now, I realize marriages in their generation seem somewhat different. They stuck with it, for the most part, regardless of the relationship. This may seem foreign in our day and time, but the covenant they made with each other is the same one we make today. Our commitment many times is not based on a feeling at all; it is simply a promise we made to each other and to our God to stick with this marriage "till death do us part." This can be much harder in the middle than it appeared in the beginning.

Through their story I learned that we need to expect overtime. It may not come in this drastic form for all of us, but it will come nonetheless. Experiences will come in our marriage when we will feel that we've given everything we have. We just know the finish line is just ahead. We just have to hang on a little longer, and then we're smacked with overtime.

It can come in the form of extended deployments, unexpected Temporary Duty (TDY) trips, a job that expects far more of our spouses than we anticipated, a delay in a Permanent Change of Station (PCS) move, a change in retirement plans, and many other ways. This overtime can even come in the form of a phone call that says they will be a few hours late coming home from the office because something came up. This request for overtime can come for just a few hours, days, months, or even years. Many times the length and reason are insignificant; sometimes it's simply overwhelming that it happens at all.

God has a plan for everything, even if it means waiting a little longer than we estimated. When overtime is called, we may think we have nothing left to give. Tears may come easy. Feelings and expectations can seem overwhelming when we're required to go a slightly adjusted or completely different direction. At this moment, we realize that we've made it this far through God's sustainment, and it is Him who will strengthen us as we go forward. We need to remember that God is in control and He has a plan for our lives. God's plan may not always turn out as we believed it would, but we'll look back someday and understand that His plan was better all along.

In dealing with these overtimes, we know the challenge has more to do with expectations than anything else. Through all of these instances, we've come to expect the end at a specified time, much like my running experience. When I run by myself, I know where I'm starting and stopping. When undertaking a training run with someone else, sometimes it's a matter of going until we're told to stop. Much of the challenge for me is managing my expectations.

Mary and Martha, Lazarus' sisters, could empathize with me, but their experience was slightly different. Lazarus and his sisters were very good friends with Jesus. In fact, He had spent some time in their home. We remember the story of Martha opening her home to Jesus. She was distracted by making preparations as Mary sat at Jesus feet (Luke 10:38–42).

Some time later, Lazarus became very ill. Mary and Martha sent word to Jesus because they knew He could heal Lazarus. Surprisingly, Jesus did not go immediately to Bethany where the three lived, but stayed another two days at His present location. By the time Jesus arrived, Lazarus had been dead four days. As Martha ran to meet Jesus, she pointed out that if Jesus had been there, Lazarus would still be alive. She knew the power that Jesus had and did not quite understand His decision to allow Lazarus to die.

Jesus comforted and assured them that He was still in control. Arriving at the tomb where they had buried Lazarus, Jesus called out to him and raised him from the dead (John 11:1–44). Once again, Jesus spent time in their home, and the three siblings, as well as others, sat and listened to His teaching. John also points out that "on account of him (Lazarus) many of the Jews were going over to Jesus and putting their faith in him" (John 12:10-11).

Talk about expectations not being met! Mary and Martha were close friends of Jesus; they knew where He was and sent messengers to tell Him Lazarus was sick. No doubt they fully expected Jesus to come running and heal Lazarus, but He didn't. He waited . . . for two days! Adding in traveling time for both the messengers and Jesus, Lazarus was dead four days before Jesus showed up. This was probably not the timetable Mary and Martha had expected. By the time Jesus arrived, they probably came to the conclusion they would not see their brother again until they met him in heaven.

Jesus had other plans. He used this opportunity for His glory. He raised Lazarus, and as a result, more people came to trust and believe in Jesus. Just think of the people who may not have believed if Jesus had done what Mary and Martha had expected. This miracle also started the chain of events that took Jesus to the cross—all because He worked off of His timetable and not theirs.

Reading the story from beginning to end, we can see God's hand on it. Living in the middle of it may have been a completely different experience. Just like the times when our expectations aren't met, it can be difficult to see God's hand at work when we're so close to the events.

Yet we have to trust Him and believe that "all things God works for the good of those who love him, who have been called according to his purpose" (Romans 8:28).

Our emotions and attitude can make overtime a struggle. We expected the deployment to end at a certain time. We expected retirement at a designated point in the future. We're always expecting something. These moments push us farther than we thought we could go, and we become stronger than we thought we could be. In 2 Corinthians 12:8-10, Paul asks God to remove a "thorn in his flesh," which is much like us asking God to bring our husband home on time or retire at the expected date. Paul pleads three times for the Lord to take the thorn away.

He shares God's reply in verse 9. "My grace is sufficient for you, for my power is made perfect in weakness." Paul explains his reaction and attitude toward this answer in the same verse. "Therefore will I boast all the more gladly about my weaknesses, so that Christ's power may rest on me."

See, just like with Mary, Martha, and Lazarus, God did not remove the challenge in Paul's life, but Paul learned to be thankful as this challenge allowed him to share even more about what God was doing in him. It allowed Paul to be more dependent on God. Had he not experienced these circumstances, Paul's faith might not have been near as strong.

Paul finishes his explanation in verse 10. "That is why, for Christ's sake, I delight in weaknesses, in insults, in hardships, in persecutions, in difficulties. For when I am weak, then I am strong." Paul had an awesome testimony! He'd learned to be thankful and to see the challenges he faced were part of a bigger plan to glorify God.

My prayer is that we look at these overtime experiences in the same light. We need to see these challenges in our lives as opportunities to share with others what Christ is doing in us, and to strengthen our faith along the way. Overtime happens when the whistle blows, a battle must still be fought, and a game must be finished. It happens when we're weary, exhausted, drained, and asked to give just a little bit more. *When* it happens, we must follow Paul's words in Colossians 2:6-7. "So then, just as you received Christ Jesus as Lord, continue to live in him, rooted and built up in him, strengthened in the faith as you were taught, and overflowing with thankfulness."

In this overtime, we need to continue trusting Christ and His guidance, learning to rest in Him. Doing this may seem difficult in such overwhelming situations, but the trick is to look back, remember what He has brought us through, and trust that He will continue with the same pattern.

Notice Paul points out that if we do this, the first thing that follows is that we are "strengthened in the faith." Trusting Christ one step at a time builds our faith and our confidence in the God we serve. Following this trust, Paul points out that our hearts should and will be overflowing with thankfulness. Hopefully, we've all experienced a time when we've seen a path God has brought us down and the purpose in it. We feel the joy and relief that He was truly in control, and we're thankful for what He's done in us up to that point, as well as His provision in the future.

As challenging as overtime can be, it's an awesome time to let Jesus shine! In these moments, our true character shows, our faith is challenged, and our weakness displayed. Yet we're also given a great opportunity to let Christ be glorified and our spiritual foundation be strengthened. Hebrews 10:39 challenges us when it says, "But we are not of those who shrink back and are destroyed, but of those who believe and are saved." God is in control, even in our most challenging moments. May we use this overtime as an opportunity for adventure and a platform to display Jesus.

We must continue to run—past the point where we started, uphill on that sometimes rocky trail, following the pace that God set for us. We must focus just as cheerleaders do, setting our minds and hearts on the task at hand. To become so engaged in our purpose that we become a sold-out part of the bigger team. This is our objective, remembering that even if the time on the scoreboard says zero, we must still wait for the final whistle. We also have to keep in mind that our husbands don't make this call. The referee's job is to decide when the game is over. God is in control.

We can do this, and in the end, we can glorify the God we serve because we did. We do not achieve this alone. God planned this all before time began, and He will be with us until it's all over. We must simply remain faithful. If we follow God's instructions, and pray with our husbands for guidance and stamina to finish, we'll be successful. We have trusted. We have believed. We have stayed true to our commitment through some difficult moments. From everyday issues to big time mountains, we've been sustained and strengthened. We've been faithful, though at times we didn't think we'd make it. Believing that God ordained our marriage, we just knew that all the effort and dedication would be worth it. We and our husbands would finish this race together. Regardless of situations encountered, we would hold on. Yet there are times, and far too many these days, when one of our friends, maybe one of our confidantes, or maybe even one of us is cut from the squad. What do we do now? How do we deal with that?

Chapter Five

Cut from the Squad

Cheerleading is a challenging proposition and it starts at young age. Children begin taking gymnastic classes and progress to cheerleading classes by the time they're in early elementary school. Once they reach high school they're ready, after years of training and practice, to tryout for the squad.

Tryouts can be scary. They require everything to be just perfect from pointed toes to smiling faces. Cheerleaders are expected to have coordination, gymnastics skills, cheer skills, and a confident personality. When they make the squad, it's exciting! They've worked and prepared for this moment. Once here, they continue to train and practice sometimes even more than before. Competitions keep their skills in tip-top shape, and making every game, sometimes even traveling long distances to do so, is an expected and required activity.

As cheerleaders, they and their families have found that this isn't a cheap commitment. They've all bought into this, with both time and money. Through fundraising, traveling, competitions, and games, cheerleading has become a way of life. The cheerleader, individually, has bought into the team for which she roots. She's become a part of a bigger plan and has committed to her role in it. She's learned to weather storms, deal with heat, soothe aching muscles, and continue smiling. The cheerleader has learned to enjoy her job, and in the process has become even better at what she does.

This is all hunky-dory until one day when she's told that she'll be cut from the squad. Whether or not she knew this day was coming is insignificant. Sometimes legitimate reasons come up that allow for this to be a fair cut, but many times no "good" reason exists. She may still go to school with the same kids. She can still even go to the games (sitting in the bleachers, of course), but she is no longer allowed to wear the uniform, use the locker rooms, or train in the team facilities any more. She's lost some of her identity and purpose. She must now make a new plan and have a new focus—not an easy task.

Some military wives have been here, as well. We've trained, worked, cheered, committed, and have still been cut from the squad. We've experienced either death or divorce, neither of which is desirable in any sense. The marriage we believed in, hoped for, and prayed through is no more. Our new circumstances leave us standing alone. For so long, our lives have consisted of orders and duty stations, and now we have neither. It's at this point that we stop to think, "What now?"

The Challenge

This chapter is my most challenging to write as it opens up my heart in ways I have never desired. I'm challenged because at one time, I was cut from the squad.

In the summer of 2002, I went to visit my family for the Fourth of July. My marine husband of almost six years had decided against going as he had some things he needed to do. My family was meeting at the lake for the weekend. Since we lived within a few hours of them, and knowing that we'd probably move within a few months, I didn't want to miss a chance to hang out with them.

I enjoyed the weekend and then headed home. Upon my arrival, I found that our other vehicle was gone, many of the things in our house were gone, and there was a note with a little money on the bed. My husband had decided that he was in love with someone else and left to be with her.

Those first few days and weeks were difficult, to say the least. Like all marriages ours was not perfect, and we'd had some recent challenges, but I had prayed and believed that God would bring us through. I knew what marriage could be. I had watched my parents work through so many things and remain faithful to each other and the God they served until my mother died. I thought for sure we would make it too. Sadly enough, I was wrong.

I struggled at first with shock, wondering how in the world someone could do such a thing. I thought surely he would come to his senses, that God would heal our hearts, and we would be able to start over. I had such faithful, godly friends, including his mother, who prayed with me and encouraged me as I worked through a range of emotions I never knew I had.

Following the initial shock, I started to wonder what was wrong with me. Surely I had done something wrong—maybe I was too chunky, maybe I complained too much, maybe I didn't do enough around the house. It took me a while to come to the understanding that his decision was exactly that—his decision. In the end, I could have been absolutely perfect, and the decision would have still been his to make.

In this process, I also had to deal with some anger. Boy, was I mad! How dare he do this!! We owned a house that still had to be paid for, a car that we still owed on, and there were so many other things that were left in my lap—and he was now multiple states away. What was I supposed to do?

In addition to that, I had been labeled a military wife for almost six years. During that time we'd been connected to a military unit at the very least, but also to the U.S. Marine Corps. This was a part of my identity. I believed that I was where God wanted me, and I really strived to be the best I could be in the role I was given as a military wife.

Those first few months were an uphill battle both spiritually and emotionally. I sat in my house, and sometimes even at work, with tears rolling down my face. I was at such a loss. In addition to the emotional toll a separation and subsequent divorce takes, to an extent, I'd also lost my identity.

During the previous six years, my focus and my objective had been on being a military wife. My mindset had been finishing an assignment or moving within a short time, always planning and looking forward to what was next. I had concentrated on getting my husband through schools and helping him prepare for deployments. Now I was supposed to figure out what I wanted to do. Where was I going to live? What job did I want to have? How was I going to pay for this? Was God going to heal this marriage?

In addition to the questions I had for myself, I also felt I had disappointed my family. As with cheerleading, when a person marries, the whole family buys in to some extent. Mine had done the same. They'd helped with the wedding, hosted us on trips home, encouraged us as we worked through schools—as well as separations, and loved us. The day I had to call my dad and explain that my husband had left broke my heart. Even more challenging was the day I had to tell him that we'd finalized the divorce—there was going to be no reconciliation. I've always hated disappointing my parents, and this was the big kahuna of all disappointments to date.

Eight months following that Fourth of July weekend, I signed the final copy of those divorce papers. The day was a sad one for me—not necessarily due to losing my husband, as I had worked through that for the most part, but in the fact that I really despised divorce and knew God was not a fan either. I believed that I had disappointed my God and my family. I felt that I had failed—big time. I hated divorce and still do, but after months of struggling with both my faith and emotions, I came to accept something I didn't completely understand. I had to now figure out what God would have me to do from here.

In the years since that time, forgiveness has covered my heart. I've also had the opportunity to see God at work and watch Him as He took a life that seemed so ugly at the time and turned it into the most beautiful blessing I could have ever imagined. I still struggle at times with feelings of failure and incompetence, but I've come to rest in the fact that God is in control, He loves me regardless, and He has taken care of so much already. Why would He not continue to do so? I'm thankful for His mercy and grace, and sometimes even (not necessarily for the circumstances I encountered) for the lessons learned along the way.

Just like cheerleaders, I had trained and sacrificed as we all do in marriage. I had attempted to learn and grow because that's exactly what is required of military wives. My family had paid a price, just as cheerleader parents do. They paid it willingly out of love, but were challenged, just like I was, when the day came that I was no longer part of the squad. Going from such a close perspective of the game to a complete outsider is a hard pill to swallow. I had bought into the game heart and soul and had no idea what to do when I was no longer fulfilling that role. God taught me many things. I share them not because we'll all go through this, but because sadly, inevitably most of us will at least know someone who will.

Recover

Cheerleaders, regardless of the reason they're cut from the squad, must do two things should they ever plan to be successful physically again—recover and train.

Recovery must come first and foremost because we won't survive the next physical challenge without it. A marathon is an excellent example. I've never run one, but I did run a half marathon once. I decided that was far enough. Running long distances like that requires a great amount of stamina and heart. But once it's over, rest becomes a vital component. I never met a smart runner who finished a long race like that one day and then went out the following day and did it again. I'm sure there are some who would, but somewhere down the road everyone's body needs time to recover.

As noted, cheerleading can also be a physically strenuous job. We probably have some old injuries that we haven't allowed to heal completely—like that ankle that gets wrapped before every game, or a knee that's still a little stiff before it's warmed up. Give it some rest. The Psalmist said it best in Psalm 46:10. "Be still, and know that I am God; I will be exalted among the nations, I will be exalted in the earth." Be still and let God do His thing. Rest in the fact that many things happen in life over which we may feel we have no control. A lot of things disappoint us and challenge us. But regardless of what comes our way, God is still God. He has a plan for every one of us. When experiencing trying circumstances, understanding God's ways may be difficult. We may ask many times why something has happened to us. Job, whose story is written in a book by the same name, would completely understand. Most of us know the story of Job in the Old Testament. He was a godly, wealthy man with a wonderful family until God stepped back and let Satan test Job. He lost everything, except his life. He did have a few close friends, although the term is used quite loosely. These friends continued to challenge him through much of his distress. They believed that surely Job had done something horrible to deserve this, or that maybe he should denounce God for allowing such things to happen.

During his trial, Job never denounced God, nor did he fall into the trap of thinking his circumstances were consequences for an unrighteous life. In fact in Job 27:5-6, Job talks to his friends and tells them, "I will never admit you are in the right; till I die, I will not deny my integrity. I will maintain my righteousness and never let go of it; my conscience will not reproach me as long as I live."

Job stayed true to his faith through all of his trials even when God did not immediately respond to him. At the end of the book, God finally talked to Job. Notice that through God's entire discourse to Job in chapters 38 through 41, He never gives Job an explanation for everything that has happened. He never gives him the answer to the question "why?" He simply reminds Job that He is God of all.

Job responds with the simple statement, "I know that you can do all things, no plan of yours can be thwarted" (Job 42:2). Job has come to rest in the fact that regardless of the circumstances, God is still in control. The cool thing is, we can rest in this fact, as well.

Job patiently waited for God's timing and trusted Him in the meantime. Job rocks. If I'd been in a similar situation, I would have been in a tizzy attempting to do all kinds of things, and I would have started believing my "friends." Job's faith held fast. He'd learned the art of waiting on God. Due to Job's faithfulness, "The Lord blessed the latter part of Job's life more than the first" (Job 42:12).

During recovery, we need to do as Job did. Though we're going through some very challenging times, we need to remember that God is in control. Just like Job, we may never know the reason why things happen, but we can know that God knew about them long ago. He wasn't taken by surprise. No matter what, He still has a plan for our lives. We need to simply rest in the fact that God is still God.

Rest is a key component in this process. This recovery time is vital to our health, but how do we accomplish it? Jesus calls us in Matthew 11:28 and says, "Come to me, all you who are weary and burdened, and I will give you rest." This is the answer. Recovery time doesn't mean quitting our lives and becoming slugs. It simply means to relax, start back at the source, and let God heal our hearts.

In order for cheerleaders to completely recover, they must also make sure that what they take into their bodies is beneficial. This includes what they drink and eat. We are no exception. In order to stay physically strong and healthy, we must make sure that our diet has all the vital components of fruits, vegetables, meat, and grains, along with plenty of water. Frequent exercise is also necessary. The healthier we are the better we feel, which drastically helps our outlook on things. Additionally, we need to make sure that what we take into our minds and hearts is also healthy material. That involves being selective about what we watch on TV, the magazines and books we read, and what we peruse on the Internet.

The friends we choose to spend time with, and the voices we listen to also play a big part in our recovery. I pray we surround ourselves with things of joy, hope, and peace—not bitterness. We tend to be very vulnerable during this time, and it's vital that everything we take in makes us healthier and stronger.

During recovery, it's important that time with Jesus is a priority and we make Him our focus. It is He who will heal us, and He who will give us rest. He can take the aches, pains, and brokenness and make us whole again. Just as He did with Job, He can bless the latter part of our lives more than the first. What awesome possibilities that holds!

Recovery is a mandatory objective in the realm of being cut from the squad. Without this time, we become fatigued, and the aches and pains we've endured become far more serious and can cause permanent injury. Keeping the mind and body healthy and focusing on the God who loves us is the best medicine for aching hearts and broken lives.

Train

We trained before we made the squad, and hopefully while serving on the squad. It doesn't stop now. This training is simply working diligently toward being exactly who God wants us to be. Peter speaks to this when he says, "So then, those who suffer according to God's will should commit themselves to their faithful Creator and continue to do good" (1 Peter 4:19). Regardless of what we've endured, God simply wants us to continue serving Him.

Peter calls us first to commitment—to our faithful Creator. Our first responsibility in this training process is to stick to what we know and the God we serve. This can be quite difficult at times. We've all started on something and had a hard time staying committed. The thing that comes to mind most for me is exercise. I love to exercise and always feel better when I do. Yet, every time I start a new kind of program or renew my desire to be more physically fit, I struggle staying with it. I start thinking of reasons why I need to sleep a little longer, or I come up with a list of other things I need to do.

Our commitment is imperative. So many times in these circumstances we expect God to give us a big picture of what our lives will look like down the road. We want to see where God wants us to go and grasp onto that vision. Rarely have I seen this happen. What I do know, is that for today God simply wants me to follow through on His direction.

We all know the basics—pray without ceasing, share fellowship with other believers, love others, and find ways to serve. The list goes on. We know to go back to where we started. We don't need a big picture or written agenda, much as we'd like to have one sometimes. God simply wants us to be faithful to what He's already called us to do—love Him and love others.

Through this step-by-step process, He graciously builds our faith and our relationship with Him so we're ready to tackle whatever might be down the road. The preparation is totally worth it and the rewards are amazing. Through this time, He also shows us little by little what He would have us do. At some time in the not-so-distant future, we'll look back and be amazed at where He has brought us because we've remained faithful in the little steps of each day.

Training in the cheerleader world requires lifting some weights, cardiovascular activity, and practicing the same stunts over and over again. We can learn some lessons from cheerleaders! Weight training for cheerleaders requires challenging themselves to lift weights they're unsure they can handle. Smart cheerleaders, just like the rest of us who work out this way, have an assistant present in the event the weight becomes too much. Usually, the trainer knows just how much individuals need to make them stronger without breaking them.

I'm sure this sounds strangely familiar. We, too, have sometimes been given a burden that we're not so sure we can handle. Our trainer, though, knows exactly what we can handle and what will make us stronger. He also stands beside us to help us . . . always. No good trainer ever walks away. They always challenge and always encourage—an awesome combination.

Joshua was afraid in his new endeavor. In Deuteronomy, Moses had come to understand that he would not enter the Promised Land with the Israelites. In Deuteronomy 31, he's "passing the torch" on to Joshua. For years, Joshua helped Moses lead the people, but now he was going to take the lead. Moses explained some things to the Israelites in order to prepare them for the journey into the Promised Land, as well as for the changeover in leadership. Once he talked to them, he brought Joshua in front of them all and spoke to him. I would bet that Joshua, even though he was a faithful man of God, might have felt some inadequacy or anxiousness at the prospect of taking the lead, especially into the Promised Land since they would have to conquer and inhabit it—not just vacation there.

As Moses talked to Joshua, he was emphatic about the duties that Joshua would perform and their importance. Following this, though, Moses spoke to Joshua as a mentor. He told him, "The Lord himself goes before you and will be with you; he will never leave you nor forsake you. Do not be afraid; do not be discouraged." (Deuteronomy 31:8)

Now, like I do at times, many may see Joshua as a patriarch, a strong faithful man of God far removed from what I am. I have to continuously remind myself, that he, too, was just a person. He had no greater skill, nor a more powerful God than the one who lives in me. Therefore, the God who went before Joshua, and would be with Joshua, is the same God who goes before me and is with me. I, too, should not be afraid or discouraged. My God is going nowhere. He'll stick with me like glue—the rubber cement kind.

How thankful I am for this fact. Because when those weights seem too heavy to bear, and when I start to feel unbalanced and weak, He's still there standing right beside me with the same encouragement and challenge. He simply wants me to trust His divine wisdom and know that He has me. He won't even look away or get distracted. The weights He gives me will make me stronger, and when I get too comfortable, He might give me just a little bit more. I can handle it, though. He knows me, He made me . . . and He knows what I can be.

Cardiovascular activity is also a mandatory part of training. This kind of training works the heart and lungs, making them both more capable in doing the job they were designed to do. It also provides us with stamina and endurance when we need it. Cardiovascular training can be accomplished in many ways based on an individual's current physical status and personal preference. Some people walk or run, some use a treadmill or elliptical, some take group exercise classes, and some even swim. Regardless of how it's accomplished, cardiovascular activity is mandatory. Through this part of training we actually lose inches; now the muscle tone acquired through weight training can actually be visible.

The same is true for us in our spiritual walk. Our cardiovascular activity requires us to keep moving and keep doing what we know we're supposed to be doing. Whether that means showing up for the job we're committed to, caring for and loving our children, or even searching for a new home and preparing to move, we continue to work at it. Accomplishing what needs to be done can be quite draining and a great struggle at times. We may be tempted to just sit in the corner and cry, wishing it would all just go away, but that's not the life God made for us. He created us for a victorious life, but the only way to do this is to use God's strength in us.

Just like when we're running, swimming, or riding a bike, we may at times have to stop for a drink or slow down to catch our breath. But we all know that if we stop when we just get a little cramp in our side, we'll never be able to go any further or grow any stronger. Sometimes we just have to push through, even if the pace is a little slower. If we push ourselves a little each time, we're amazed at how far we can really go! We need to take the strength of our Savior and set about doing what He has called us to do.

At this challenging juncture in life, just maintaining can be a struggle. We know, though, what we need to be doing. Just like when we engage in normal cardiovascular activity, we'll have times when we're tired and our knees hurt. A periodic break or time of rest is never bad in and of itself. The downfall is when we don't get back up and keep going, trusting that God knows our limitations and He'll take us where He wants us to go.

This leads us to the last area of training. In order to truly be ready for what's out there, cheerleaders must also practice their stunts—the same ones—over and over. The repetition is what makes them good at it. Dare I say we do the same? Sometimes repetition gets really old. Trying something new seems like such a great idea, and truth be told it's not always a bad idea, but to be successful, we must be really good at something.

Growing up, I played a lot of different sports and tried a lot of other extracurricular activities. I was pretty good at most of them, but in none of them was I ever the best. This is the story of my athletic career. I was always competitive, but never number one. I believe the reason didn't necessarily lie in the fact that I lacked certain skills, was the wrong size, or wasn't fast enough. I believe that it quite possibly lay in the fact that I never fully concentrated on one area and gave everything I had to it. I much preferred to do multiple things and simply be mediocre.

God has not called us to be mediocre at all. He's called us to specific tasks and asked that we focus our time, attention, and energy on those things. Much like my athletic life, I sometimes try to dip my hand into too many things, or try to predict what God might want me to do next and jump right out there ahead of Him. We can all see the brilliance in that idea, but I try it anyway. God has given us certain skills and abilities that He wants us to use along with the basic expectations of all Christians. His requirement of us is to continue working at those specific things to which He's called us already and leave the planning and creativity of the masterpiece of our lives to Him.

Personally, as I reflect on my success in the athletic arena, I'm inclined to think God's way of doing things is far better than mine. Profound, I know. He simply wants me to perform those same stunts over and over again. Not to be bored, but to see the difference I can make when I've learned to perfect and use the special things He gave only to me. If I don't learn to use those things to His glory, no one else can do it for me. He didn't give all those abilities to anyone else. So might I suggest we take a cue from the cheerleader training and continue to work at those stunts to which He has already called us?

Being cut from the squad, regardless of reason, can be overwhelming and heart-breaking, I know. We can feel lost, inadequate, tired, hurt, and burdened, and yet all of our circumstances are no surprise to the God who made us. He still has a plan for us, a purpose and a destiny He scheduled long before we even walked this planet. He loves us more than any human could, and He has the awesome ability to stay with us ALL the time. Relax and focus on Him, and Him alone. Trusting Him to care for us, guide us, and give us direction—all of which we desperately need.

God has truly blessed my life since that time I was cut from the squad. Had you asked me eight years ago where I would be today, I couldn't have imagined standing here. I am now married to a godly man. We have two beautiful children. And strangely enough, I am again a military wife. I've been blessed beyond measure. Remarriage is not God's plan for everyone. But make no mistake, God has a plan . . . for each of us. My prayer is that we'll all seek and find the purpose for which God has created us and pursue that with passion—and just watch God take care of the rest. Prepare to be WOWED!

"Trust in the Lord with all your heart and lean not on your own understanding; in all your ways acknowledge him, and he will make your paths straight" (Proverbs 3:5-6). What awesome advice! We must trust in our Savior, commit our ways to Him, and allow Him to take us where He would have us go. I can't wait to see where we end up . . . only by the grace of God.

At times we're cut from the squad, but we may also encounter times when we're required to change squads. This means different uniforms, expectations, and possibly location, but it also means cheering for a completely different team. Our husbands at some time will change teams whether at retirement or at the end of their commitment. We'll go with them. Changing squads can be intimidating, but it can also be the adventure of a lifetime for us and our husbands. Look out civilians, here we come!

Chapter Six

Pom-poms of a Different Color

The color of a cheerleader's pom-poms is the tell-tale sign of which team she supports. Matching uniforms and identical pom-poms give the squad distinctiveness; it sets them apart from other squads and ties them to the team they support. These tangible objects become items of pride and symbols of unity.

Cheerleaders, through years of training and performing, have learned a lot about each other and the team they support. They've learned to work together and depend on each other. They've also developed an attachment to the team for which they root, and achieved some loyalty and fondness for both the individual players and the team as a whole. As they grow in age and skill, cheerleaders inevitably change squads. They may move up from middle to high school or from a junior varsity to a varsity squad. In some of these transitions, they'll experience some similarities as they may be in the same school or have other cheerleaders move with them. But the time will inevitably come when they must change pom-pom colors by themselves.

This change can be intimidating as it means adjusting to new surroundings, learning new ways of training, memorizing new cheers, and getting along with new personalities, all of which requires some courage and confidence. They must find how they fit in with this new squad and learn to use their uniqueness to make it even better. Entering these uncharted waters can be daunting, but each cheerleader must remember the skills they've been taught and the training they've received, and continue to pursue excellence.

This transition can present obvious challenges. Not only does the cheerleader change squads, they change game locations, mascots, and team colors. They learn to train differently, and the traditions of this new team will probably be unique, as well. They may use different cheers, different skills, and have different expectations.

With so many differences, they can lose sight of the fact that they're only expected to do their very best. They must focus on the basic skills they've learned along the way and then open up to learn a plethora of new ones. The transition can be a challenge, but these differences are exactly what they need to make them stronger. The challenge is what makes them grow. Regardless of what our husbands do for a living, we're asked to cheer for them. This is a wonderful opportunity and, at times, quite a challenge. Changing pom-pom colors can be a big deal—especially in the military world. Our pom-poms change colors due to our husbands' discharge from the military, whether after their original contract completion or at retirement. Either way it happens, we're required to adjust and change our loyalties. For the most part, we military wives have achieved a level of devotion and have adjusted to the expectations of this olive-drab world. Changing squads can sometimes be challenging as we integrate into a completely different environment in the civilian sector—not better or worse, just different.

Changing teams doesn't mean it's time to retire our positions as cheerleaders. Our pom-poms change colors, but our responsibilities are the same. Married to the man God has given us, we cheer for the same individual. His jersey is just not the same color—nor is the mascot or game location the same. We find that our loyalty is not necessarily to the color of our pom-poms, but to the players themselves—or one player in particular. So regardless of the team or location, we continue to fulfill the responsibility we've been given.

As with cheerleaders, this change can require some adjustment. We get accustomed to our location or the team we support. Many of us enjoy military life. And even if we would have chosen something different, we've acclimated to the environment. The adjustment to new surroundings, and even a new family in the civilian world, can be a struggle. It affects us in every way from healthcare to housing. Sometimes finding where God wants to plant us in this stage of our lives is a test in itself. The cool thing is that even though many things may change—location, friends, church, pom-pom colors—we're still married to the man God gave us. This change is actually a wonderful opportunity to try new things and "choose your own adventure."

While our husbands serve in the military, many of our moves and life-changes are due to the needs of the organization we serve, although I truly believe that God ordains it all. When we leave that world, we have a whole new adventure ahead. As a little girl, I loved reading books where I could choose my own adventure. I thought it was so cool that I could decide how the story would go. Even cooler was the fact that I could choose multiple times. I didn't have to make only one decision to determine the entire rest of the story. I was able to make multiple decisions along the way, continuing along the same path or changing my direction completely.

This change in pom-pom color gives us and our husbands, as a team, the opportunity to do just that! Leaving military life can sometimes feel like culture shock, possibly causing some anxiety as we step out into the unknown. We and our husbands are now deciding what to do with the rest of our lives. We get to pick the location, the job . . . everything! This decision-making can be awesome and it can be overwhelming, but what an adventure we have before us. And it's one that we get to create!

When searching for direction and strength, the Psalms seem to provide what I need. Two verses in particular talk about this adventure. The first one speaks about trust, but also the need for us to put forth some effort. "Commit your way to the Lord; trust in him and he will do this: He will make your righteousness shine like the dawn" (Psalm 37:5-6). The second refers to God's guidance, which is a gift. "For this

God is our God for ever and ever; he will be our guide even to the end"
(Psalm 48:14).

What wonderful promises in this new adventure! If we commit our
ways to Him and trust Him, He'll guide us. I love how the Psalmist
makes it very personal by saying, "this God is our God." He is truly
that—our God. We have no better reason to trust and worship Him
than the fact that He is God. As we set out on this adventure, how great
is it to know that He'll guide us "even to the end."

God has a plan for our families. He's already mapped out where
He wants us to go and how He wants us to get there. "For I know the
plans I have for you," declares the Lord, "plans to prosper you and not
to harm you, plans to give you a hope and a future. Then you will call
upon me and come and pray to me, and I will listen to you. You will
seek me and find me when you seek me with all your heart." (Jeremiah
29:11-13)

We must learn in these times to reach out to Him in faith and let
Him speak to our hearts. These decisions may seem overwhelming, but
that is exactly why God gives us answers in smaller portions. He becomes
the most important part of choosing our adventure, reaching down and
showing us the next step to take. We then have the opportunity to
follow or not, our choice. Years from now when we look back at the
little steps we've taken along the way and see how far God has brought
us, we'll be amazed.

This new adventure will be an exciting one, but we must remember
through all of these decisions where our priorities lie. First and foremost,
God wants all of us, soul, mind, and strength, in service to Him. Loving
and serving Christ is our ultimate goal in whatever we do in life and
this step along the path is no exception. God specifies this in Jeremiah
when He said, "you will seek me and find me *when* you seek me with
all of your heart" (Jeremiah 29:13). Seeking with all of our heart is the
caveat to success; half-hearted seeking gets us nowhere.

Our second priority should be to our spouse. After our call to
Christ, our second calling is to our spouses as we have become one with
them, and therefore, ideally will operate as such. We are in this together,

but ultimately we should submit first to Christ's will and then to our husbands' decisions. Submission, although a touchy subject, becomes a matter of high priority in the success of our adventure.

Submission

We would have addressed this earlier, but it didn't seem to fit as well anywhere else. The idea of submission, especially to a human being with all his faults and issues, is a sensitive subject in today's world, but one that I believe is of critical importance. Christ discusses this multiple times in His Word. Peter wrote to the Ephesians, "Wives, submit to your husbands as to the Lord. For the husband is the head of the wife as Christ is head of the church, his body, of which he is the Savior. Now as the church submits to Christ, so also wives should submit to their husbands in everything" (Ephesians 5:22-24).

Okay, take a deep breath.

The first time I remember reading these words as a wife my initial thought was that the Bible was comparing my husband to Jesus. This comparison was not necessarily one I would have made. As much as I love the man, this was a bit of a stretch. Once I got past that first reaction, I began to understand the analogy. Christ, as head of the church, has left the opportunity open for the church to walk away from Him. It's that little thing called "free will." No matter what sacrifices Jesus made or how much love He shows us, our submission to Him as a church is completely voluntary. The same is true with regard to submission of the wife to the husband—completely voluntary. I like the idea of having a choice. But as we know with Christ and the church, submission can be awesome! Being able to rest in Christ, knowing that He loves us as much as He does, and that He knows all is a gigantic relief of a burden. We can just let Him handle the problems and challenges, and give us the direction we need. He does allow us to talk to Him, share our hearts, and serve Him, even in the little things.

I know what crossed my mind when I first studied this. If my husband were as perfect as Christ, submission would be a piece of cake.

But as we have all found out in our Christian walk, even submission to Christ is a struggle for us at times and He's the God of the universe. Granted, our husbands may not have given their lives for us lately, and they certainly don't know the right answer for everything, but God has given them to us nonetheless and commanded us to submit to the authority He has given them.

Notice, if we go back and read Ephesians 5:22–33, that God referenced the act of submission by the wife before He explained the role of the husband. I used to think that if my husband acted the way he was supposed to, then I would submit to him as I was expected. The problem with that thought is neither the actions of the wife nor the husband are in any way dependent upon the actions of the other. Put another way, I'm commanded to submit to my husband and let God take care of whatever my husband does. My submission to him is actually a submission to God. It's an act of faith knowing that God is in control of everything.

Peter talks about submission from a little bit different perspective.

> Wives, in the same way be submissive to your husbands so that, if any of them do not believe the word, they may be won over without words by the behavior of their wives, when they see the purity and reverence of your lives. Your beauty should not come from outward adornment, such as braided hair and the wearing of gold jewelry and fine clothes. Instead, it should be that of your inner self, the unfading beauty of a gentle and quiet spirit, which is of great worth in God's sight. For this is the way the holy women of the past who put their hope in God used to make themselves beautiful. They were submissive to their own husbands, like Sarah, who obeyed Abraham and called him her master. You are her daughters if you do what is right and do not give way to fear (1 Peter 3:1-6).

When we look at submission from this perspective, it has a far greater purpose. The act in itself becomes our way to minister to those around us, as well as display the true beauty within us. How thankful I am that my husband can see this true beauty, because anything I had in the physical realm is becoming increasingly aged.

We also notice the reference to Sarah. Amazingly enough, she can relate to exactly how we feel as military wives. We remember the story of when God called Abraham, or Abram as he was called at the time (Genesis 12:1-3). The whole story of Abram and Sarai is amazing anyway, but this particular instance is when God called Abram to an unknown land—later to be called the Promised Land, to which the Israelites would return. "The Lord had said to Abram, 'Leave your country, your people and your father's household and go to the land I will show you'" (Genesis 12:1).

Two points intrigue me in this one verse. First of all, we notice that God said this to Abram. Nowhere does it say that God said anything about this move to Sarai. As military wives, we can surely relate. Abram comes home and tells her that God told him they were to move—to an unknown land. This is not a comparison of God to the army, or any other branch of service for that matter, but it's nice to know that I'm not alone in this experience of having my husband tell me it's time to move.

Apparently, Sarai trusted Abram—and God—and off she went with her husband. Nowhere in scripture does it say that Abram discussed the idea with his wife or that Sarai questioned Abram at all. I have no doubt they discussed it, but Sarai amazes me. She packed up their entire household, said goodbye to the people and places she'd known all her life, and went.

The second point that intrigues me is the fact that God didn't tell them where they were going. I've had many experiences moving or submitting to God's plan for our family, but there has always been a plan. I'm impressed that Sarah and Abram would pack up everything (including taking along some of their relatives) and just head out in the direction God pointed, clueless to their destination. The faith they must have had to take God at His word and follow the call He placed on their lives, knowing that He would provide for them along the way. My prayer is that I can have such faith.

Our daughter recently challenged us in exactly this area. As we were reading stories about what the church is doing, from providing disaster relief to planting new churches for specific people groups, our daughter looked at us and said, "Maybe we should be missionaries."

I explained to her that technically we're all considered missionaries, some of us just go to foreign lands and some of us stay, but we're all called to be missionaries. I initially thought she didn't understand what it takes to provide for a family. She didn't comprehend the necessity of finding a place to live, feeding our family, and providing an education for our children—all very important things. As I thought about the conversation, though, I desired to have childlike faith again. In her mind, our duty was to do whatever Christ called us to do—period, and let Him take care of the rest. She was right.

Submission works much the same way for me. I want to follow through on God's calling, but then I also want a back-up plan. Needing a back-up plan for God is ridiculous, I know, but I try to have one anyway. God doesn't want that at all. He wants whole-hearted surrender to Him. That's all He asks, and yet I have such a hard time doing that very thing.

Submission has been a challenging lesson for me. I believe in my husband and think he's a wonderful man, but sometimes I want to do things my way, or at least know the complete plan before heading out in any direction.

My most poignant example took place when my husband purchased a motorcycle. We bought it believing it was what he wanted. But the motorcycle didn't enable him to do the kind of driving he desired. This led to a discussion about trading in the current bike for a different one. The one we had was paid off, and acquiring another would require us to go into debt again—not a fun subject with me.

Tears were involved as we sat around the kitchen island and talked about the best course of action to take. It was a big moment for me when I took a deep breath and told my husband that I trusted him. If he believed this was the right thing to do for our family, I would defer to his judgment. We acquired the new bike.

To this day, I don't know why God brought this decision to us. Amazingly enough, we don't even own the bike anymore. We sold the new one less than a year later to have extra money for some retirement property. The lesson may well have been simply to work on my submission. Regardless of the purpose, the lesson I learned was huge. I had to learn to take a deep breath, pray diligently, and trust that my husband would follow God's leading. I also came to peace with the understanding that even if my husband does not follow God's plan exactly every time, which is quite possible considering he's human, God is still in control.

Now, how does this tangent tie into changing the color of our pom-poms? We need to understand that our loyalty must first reside with our God and second with our husband. This road will be an interesting one as we enter a new chapter of life, but we must stick together as a team and learn to serve God in a new capacity. We must also continue in the God-given responsibilities of supporting and encouraging our husbands, and also finding God's area of service for us in this new place.

It says in 1 Peter 3:6, "You are her daughters if you do what is right and do not give way to fear." Fear is something I completely understand, and releasing control can stir it within me. Peter reminds us, though, that we need to do what's right and not give way to that fear. We have to rest in the faith that God will catch us every time. Peter says we are her (Sarai's) daughters if we follow this course of action. How amazing was she? She trusted her husband and ultimately her God enough to follow without fear to an unknown destination.

Some of our decisions will be quite difficult. All of them, to be successful, will require a unanimous vote. Many times I've wanted to jump ahead and tell my husband what I think God wants him or us to do in certain areas. I've come to the astounding conclusion that this doesn't work very well. First of all, my husband is gracious (and brilliant) and asks for my opinion most of the time when making decisions. I really appreciate this, except when he doesn't follow my advice. I get a little over confident at times and think my answer is the only way. This never seems to work very well either. I have yet to achieve the "unfading beauty of a gentle and quiet spirit" (1 Peter 3:4).

God has called each of us to serve different roles in our homes. Being in charge is not the role He gave me. He put the responsibility of leading our family in following God's path on my husband's shoulders . . . as well as the consequences of not following. This isn't a "glad I am not you!" moment because God has given me my own responsibilities. This simply allows me to stand back, offer my opinion when asked, pray diligently for my husband and our family, and seek God's will in it all.

Allowing us each to take on the role God has given us, gives us a freedom to be exactly who He wants us to be. Additionally, we come to understand God is actually in control. How thankful I am! I also love the structure that God has given our home as it allows it to function as God intended and therefore, makes us far more successful in reaching others for Christ, which is our ultimate objective.

Teamwork

Submission is an amazing thing. It leads us into a wonderful relationship with our husbands. We begin to form our own team. And after years of working together to accomplish what God has set out for us to do, we have ideally joined together truly as one in heart and mind. We've learned to live in the unity that God intended for us, and the experience is awesome. Few of us live in this ideal world all of the time, though.

Teamwork is imperative. My husband and I would love to hang out in the perfect world with the perfect marriage all of the time. Alas, in order to accomplish that objective we'd both need to be perfect . . . not a likely possibility any time soon. But we've learned to form a foundation, and then use that foundation to build a life.

Our foundation, as you have likely guessed, is the relationship we have with our Savior. Since that is securely in place, we have basically formed a mission statement or family objective. Silly as it may sound, this concept is very much like corporations. The mission of the corporation allows its employees to make independent decisions, but still keep the company on the right track.

Our marriage is much the same at times. We've determined that our objective is to reach people for Christ, usually through acts of service. This extends to financial, time management, and any other decisions that may come up along the way. Before we go too far, let me reiterate the fact that my husband and I do actually talk to each other regularly. And when it comes to big decisions, we make those together—usually with lots of prayer involved. We've found that with mutual foundations and objectives, we communicate far more efficiently, and we frequently find ourselves going in the same direction anyway. We've learned to trust, but to also keep each other accountable as we travel through this life.

When developing a team, communication is vitally important. Regardless of the direction we take, we need to take it together. My husband is a "leave and cleave" kind of guy. He refers frequently to Genesis 2:24 where God has created Adam and Eve. The Bible states that "a man will leave his father and mother and be united to his wife." We love our families dearly. We have awesome parents and siblings, but we firmly believe that God has now given us each other and has a plan for us. As much as we appreciate advice and help from our extended families, we are ultimately responsible for the choices we make for our immediate family. Together we make up our team—along with our children for now.

God frequently asks us to do things that require stepping out in faith. We figuratively and literally join hands and jump off the diving board of life together. While standing on the edge of the diving board preparing to jump, we look down and think for sure this is more like cliff jumping than stepping off of a diving board. The feeling is a little scary. The water looks much farther down from here than it did when we stood on the side of the pool. But we've discovered that if we jump together, the water isn't really as far as it seems. The cliff is just a diving board after all, and the landing is much softer than I imagined. Just think what we would've missed if we'd never taken that first step—the exhilaration of the jump or the coolness of the water—experiences that can't be replicated.

In all of these circumstances, when God challenged us a little more than what we thought we could handle, He's never pushed us too far, too fast, or risked our safety. He's created a plan that is best for us because the plan involves furthering the kingdom. When we follow His leading and trust Him, we find that our life is phenomenal. We might not be wealthy or famous, but we're exactly where we're supposed to be—and no better place exists on the planet.

We're learning to rely on each other and the God we serve in order to fulfill the responsibilities that God has ordained for us. We must grow spiritually and allow God to challenge us, having faith in the path He has set. We join hands with each other and realize that God has a destiny for us . . . and we can't wait to see where He takes us!

We must work together. Teamwork is imperative. We have to be committed for life, otherwise teamwork fails—and so does the plan. We learn to trust each other, see and use each other's strengths, build up each other's weaknesses, remain wholly devoted to prayer for each other and our families, remember to love each other as Christ loved us, and hang on for the ride. My husband and I are still learning and working toward such lofty goals, and we pray the same for every military couple, especially as they face a change in pom-pom color. All we need now is a family cheer!

The shift from military to civilian life creates an amazing number of decisions. The choices we have will be interesting, and what an adventure! Together with our husbands, we've ideally achieved a workable team. Even if the teamwork is not completely successful, we know the God in charge, and we know what He can accomplish. We acquired awesome skills and abilities during our time as military wives. These are great attributes we can share wherever God plants us. We should be a great asset to our new squad.

Acquiring pom-poms of a different color is also a great opportunity for both us and our husbands to seek God again and come together in the excitement of this new adventure. He has a plan set out for us. Remember, though, that a new squad may mean a new position or responsibility than we had in the last squad. It may also mean different training regimens and new traditions. Be prepared to adjust and use what God has given us in a new capacity. We must be willing to open our hearts to whatever God may have in store and enjoy the ride! We need not be intimidated by the changes we'll face, but use those changes to make us stronger. What a great opportunity for God to mold us into a little bit more of what He would have us be.

The transition is a drastic one, but not insurmountable. We've already survived making huge adjustments—from changing houses to changing continents—and have been successful. We've seen how God has brought us from one place to another and are able to look back at all that God has done in our lives as we go from place to place. Reflecting on faces of friends strewn around the world brings back many memories. We remember our first house, as well as the home where the kids learned to walk. We reminisce about the neighbors along the way, the crazy weather we experienced, the balls and parties, and the history created over a couple of years or over a lifetime. With God's help, we've accomplished so much, and now God is taking us down another fork in the road. Oh, the adventure ahead! This change in pom-pom color will be awesome. You'll see. So cheer on!

Speaking of cheering, we've come to the time of celebration. We've battled the weather, learned and trained as best we could, possibly fought through some injuries, and maybe even been cut from the squad. Whether we're still military wives or have transitioned to civilian life, we have cause to rejoice. In our reflection of what God has brought us through, we remember also the victories, the joyful celebration of God's grace. And celebrate we must!

Chapter Seven

Touchdown!

TOUCHDOWN!!! Woohoo!! Time to dance! Choreographed or not, the moment the ball enters the end zone it's time to celebrate! Whether it entered from an interception run sixty-five yards or the offensive line pushed through that last half yard with pure grit, the result is the same. Starting with the players on the field, moving to the players on the sidelines and the cheerleaders just beyond them, a ripple of celebration makes its way to the top of the bleachers. Playing the fight song with unwavering devotion, the band accompanies the joy of a school united. The announcer in the box even uses all of his self-control to proclaim the achievement without yelling into his microphone. This moment is the culmination of hours of training, many motivational speeches, and sheer determination.

Although a little chaotic, the excitement is contagious. The most interesting displays of animation are the players who seem to have choreographed a routine for just this moment in time. I can't help but wonder how they created their dance and where in the world they must have practiced. Though at times the routine seems silly, the players show a characteristic I truly believe God wants in all of us—the ability to throw off our inhibitions and celebrate everything He's done, and all the things He has yet to do. He wants us to dance because we serve a great God and we can't contain the excitement.

When the ball crosses into the end zone, the path taken to get there becomes inconsequential, as do the numbers on the scoreboard. The touchdown represents a celebration of a sought-after objective and renewed hope, bringing to light all of the possibilities the future may hold. The celebration is an affirmation of the teamwork involved, as well as a display of unity for an entire school. This moment is unlike any other, and yet, in a true struggle for victory, the celebration at times comes in terms of yards and not simply touchdowns.

Celebrate!

Every one of us has touchdowns we can celebrate. Some of these celebrations happen annually, like birthdays and anniversaries. Others are more infrequent, like promotions. Regardless of their frequency, we celebrate these touchdowns every time because they signify milestones and victories. Much like in football, these touchdowns are the result of goals obtained and renewed hope for the future. They are wonderful moments we cherish for a lifetime.

Celebration is a popular topic in the Bible. God commanded the Israelites to celebrate multiple festivals throughout the Old Testament, usually as a reminder of what God had done for them throughout history. Jesus also talked about celebration when He told the parable of the lost son (Luke 15:11-32) and ended with the words, "But we had to celebrate and be glad, because this brother of yours was dead and is alive again; he was lost and is found" (Luke 11:32). Using this illustration, God showed exactly what happens in heaven when we come to Him for forgiveness. The psalmist calls us to celebrate, as well, when he says, "They will celebrate your abundant goodness and joyfully sing of your righteousness" (Psalm 145:7).

All of these instances—and many more—demonstrate the importance of celebration. Beyond birthdays, anniversaries, and promotions, we encounter other times in our lives when we see tangible victory, feel the providential hand of protection, and experience true joy. These are moments when God's abundant goodness washes over us and we can joyfully sing. We celebrate because our hearts overflow with happiness, and we can't help but praise the God who is responsible.

We see these touchdown moments in our lives and others. Moments when marriages are reconciled, someone gives their life to the Savior, physical healing takes place, and many other instances when we stand back in awe of what God can do. The ripple effect starts at the end zone and reaches the top of the bleachers as a deafening roar overtakes the stadium. These moments bring unity, fill us with joy, provide renewed hope, and overwhelm us with peace. These are our touchdowns!

Celebrating them is mandatory, but it's also something we can't help. Whether we celebrate with balloons and parties, or shouts of joy and high fives is insignificant. We just need to celebrate. This joyful exuberance allows us to praise the God who made the touchdown possible, join with our families or other believers in unity, and display to the world the love and faithfulness of a holy God.

First Down

Most of us would agree that in real life, as in football, celebrations should sometimes come more in terms of yards than touchdowns. We all have times in life when we beat ourselves against the line of scrimmage, and every yard is taken by sheer determination. We press on in what feels like the battle of the underdog hoping to survive. In these times, each yard forward, each first down is a time worth celebrating.

My most vivid recollection of such a time happened my first summer as a children's resident camp director; the first three weeks were more than I could bear. I had visited the emergency room with a child or staff person at least every other day for everything from a kidney stone to a bloody nose, two of my staff had come perilously close to endangering the lives of some children, and my marriage was struggling.

On the first day of week four, an irate parent called me to share that the bus was a few minutes late picking up her child and she had to wait in the rain. At that moment, I had experienced maximum capacity for craziness. I graciously informed the parent that she could wait for the bus in her car and called my boss.

In the phone call, I explained that I no longer desired to hold my job. I asked him to come out to camp so that I could leave immediately. He asked where I planned to go; I had no idea. All I knew was that I no longer wanted to be there. He came to my rescue, but not as I had expected. He didn't allow me to quit, but held my hand, almost literally, for the next few days while he took over my job and let me just follow him around. Eventually, he went back to his camp and I finished the summer, and a subsequent summer, successfully. I learned through the experience to get up every day and start over, to be thankful at the end of the day when everything went mostly right, and that sometimes it really helps if someone holds my hand for awhile.

That one experience taught me most of all that celebrations sometimes need to occur for the yardage gained each day or even at times for holding the line of scrimmage. The times when we struggle most are the exact times that we need to celebrate the little things along the way. If we contemplated and tried to number all that God has done in our lives, from the provision of food to the safety of our children, we'd soon lose count of the blessings. The individual care He takes for each of us and the love and grace He daily displays are beyond our understanding, but can overwhelm us with peace.

God desires for us to celebrate and rejoice, even during the difficult times. Philippians 4:4 tells us to, "Rejoice in the Lord always, I will say it again: Rejoice!" Notice we are called to rejoice in the Lord—not in our circumstances or in the people around us, but in our Savior.

This time of celebration may lack balloons and streamers, but it is no less significant. God continues to provide and sustain, giving us strength and hope for tomorrow. During this time, we can also look back at what He has done and rejoice in where He has brought us.

In football, we watch as our team completes a pass or a runner finds a hole in the defense and picks up some major yardage. We get excited watching the huge leaps of success as they strive for the end zone, but we also experience with them their struggles to make a gain of even a yard. When nothing seems to work as it should, and we watch the team pound against the defensive line exhausted and overwhelmed, we suffer with them. So as best we can, we continue providing support and encouragement from the sidelines.

During moments when we can only cheer in support, we cheerleaders understand; we have those days too. Cheerleaders, just like players, have days when they're sore and fatigued or their stunts aren't working as planned. Days when they repeat the same stunt over and over, yet they still can't land it. Days when they get to the end of a cheer and can't stick the "ta-da!" at the end.

I've felt like that cheerleader many times when the weather was great, the team wasn't doing badly, but for some reason, I was just off. Nothing seemed to work the way it was intended, and I felt ready for the game to be over so I could try it again the following day.

In those moments, as we do with the players, we have to learn to celebrate the accomplishments, as minute as they may be, and rejoice in where God has brought us. Instead of hoping to survive and waiting until the next game or next season, we have to set our minds to enjoy the abundance God has set out for us that day.

Jesus said, "The thief comes only to steal, kill, and destroy; I have come that they may have life, and have it to the full" (John 10:10). Satan's plan is to thwart the abundant life God gave us and talk us into just surviving or waiting until a better time comes. God's desire was not for us to have abundant life periodically, but to live in such a state all the time, to live abundantly in all circumstances, to be victorious today.

The celebrations become less about the yardage gained or the score on the scoreboard. They focus more on the strength, perseverance, and without a doubt, the awesome grace of our heavenly Father. We come to realize that the celebration is not about us at all, but about glorifying God and sharing with the world all He has done. Isn't that how our entire lives are supposed to be, though? All about Jesus.

Anticipation

As normal humans, we've learned to celebrate the things we can see and the events we understand like birthdays, promotions, and salvation. But I believe God would have us celebrate what He has yet to do, as well. We know what God has done to this point and some of the things He can do, although He still surprises me, but we forget to look forward with anticipation to what He's *going* to do.

I know this may sound crazy since most of us have no idea what He's going to do next. The thought, though, is not that we know *what* God is going to do, but that we know He's going to do *something*. We can celebrate the fact that God loves us and cares for us, and joyfully anticipate what He'll do next. I get excited about such thoughts. I love seeing what happens next, because I've found that in all my attempts at dreaming up outcomes, they never seem to compare to what God actually does.

Amazingly, God pointed out this very fact in Ephesians 3:20-21. "Now to him who is able to do immeasurably more than we could ask or imagine, according to his power that is at work within us, to him be glory in the church and in Christ Jesus throughout all generations, for ever and ever! Amen." He can do way more than what I can dream up, and I plan to celebrate the outcome in faith, knowing that God will take care of everything.

God even asked the Israelites to celebrate what was to come. In Exodus 12, God gave Moses directions for the celebration of the Passover. The Israelites were living in Egypt as slaves during this time and God had sent Moses to lead the people out of Egypt into the Promised Land. Up to this point, Moses had talked to Pharaoh as God had commanded him; God even sent nine plagues upon the land of Egypt, but Pharaoh still refused to free the Israelites.

In Exodus 11, God explains the tenth plague, that of the firstborn, to Moses. God then calls the people to celebrate the outcome of this plague in Exodus 12:1-28, even though it had yet to actually happen. The plague, as you might remember, was that the Lord would pass through Egypt during the night and strike down the firstborn in the land, both people and animals.

To keep the Israelites from experiencing this tragedy, God instructed them to put lamb's blood on the top and sides of the doorframes of their houses. They were also supposed to be dressed to leave, with the expectation that through this plague, Pharaoh would free them. The blood would allow the Lord to pass over their home and keep the destructive plague from touching their families.

That is exactly what happened. The Israelites followed the instructions, and the plague affected all of the Egyptian families and their livestock, but passed over the Israelites. Pharaoh then kicked the Israelites out of Egypt in the middle of the night. The Israelites were prepared and left immediately.

Can you imagine what the conversation was like in the Israelite homes that night? I would bet nobody went to sleep; they were much too excited to see what God was going to do. They had celebrated God's deliverance while still captives, believing that God would save them . . . and He did. They were instructed to continue celebrating this Passover, even after they entered the Promised Land, in order to teach future generations about the power and provision of God.

This story amazes me, not simply in the care God took to protect His people, but in the call to celebrate something that had not yet taken place. It's likely that the people didn't completely understand all of the specifics of God's plan. When Moses and Aaron explained the celebration and the Lord's instructions, the Israelites "bowed down and worshiped. The Israelites did just what the Lord commanded Moses and Aaron" (Exodus 12:27b-28). They didn't question the instructions or the outcome; they bowed down and worshiped.

I believe God wants the same from us. We may not have the specific instructions He gave the Israelites or a heads-up to the outcome, but we can celebrate nonetheless, believing that He who promised is faithful. We know He's able to do anything, He loves us beyond our comprehension, and He knows far more about the current situation and its impact on eternity than we do. Why would we not want to celebrate? Even if our prayers are not answered the way we desire, or the conclusion is not what we would have chosen, we know that the intent of all things is to bring glory to God. We can celebrate because we believe in the end the spotlight will be on Jesus, exactly where it should be.

Do the Dance

Celebrations, whether for touchdowns, gains in yardage, or holding the line of scrimmage, are times to dance. Watching celebrations from the bleachers, I've many times sat in awe of players' lack of inhibitions on the field. It took me years to be comfortable doing such dances in the kitchen of my own house, much less in front of hundreds or thousands of spectators.

The players, though, freely do the jig they created without concern for those watching, including the cameras that record every move. This, I believe, is what God wants from us. Not necessarily to dance a jig in front of thousands of people, but to openly and unashamedly celebrate the God we serve.

King David rocked at this. In 2 Samuel 6, we read about David bringing the Ark of the Covenant to Jerusalem. On their journey from Abinadab's house, David and thirty thousand chosen men of Israel walked in front of the Ark as it traveled, "celebrating with all their might before the Lord, with songs and with harps, lyres, tambourines, sistrums and cymbals" (2 Samuel 6:5). Later, David "danced before the Lord with all his might" (2 Samuel 6:14).

Throwing off all inhibitions, David celebrated the Lord he loved so much, even to the dismay of those around him. In fact, his wife Michal, "when she saw King David leaping and dancing before the Lord, she despised him in her heart" (2 Samuel 6:16). David knew what he was doing, though. "David said to Michal, 'It was before the Lord, who chose me rather than your father or anyone from his house when he appointed me ruler over the Lord's people Israel—I will celebrate before the Lord'" (2 Samuel 6:21).

David knew who was in charge and what God had done in him, and he worshiped. David was frequently celebrating and rejoicing, even to the embarrassment of his wife at times, but he rejoiced regardless, because he was truly thankful. We should get excited when we reflect on what God has done and look with anticipation at what God can do down the road. David shared his desire for others to experience this attitude of rejoicing in Psalm 68:3 when he said, "But may the righteous be glad and rejoice before God; may they be happy and joyful."

I believe David truly understood the importance of rejoicing and being thankful, partially because he understood what an awesome God he had and partially because he had been on the other side of mourning, whether due to the loss of a loved one or through his own disobedience. He had experienced grief and repentance. Out of this experience, though, he also saw God's grace and provision, and he rejoiced. He saw first-hand the love God had for him and for his people.

David was not unique in this way. He experienced the same trials, heartaches, and mistakes that we do. He simply opened his eyes and heart to his God and saw God's hand on it all. We can do the same. We can see the struggles and challenges, but we can also see God's hand at work. Even if we don't see His hand at the time, we can know that He's there because He's *promised* to be there, and has always *been* there before. We are showered with grace, peace, and hope regardless of our actions or circumstances. This, in itself, is cause for rejoicing.

Now, do I plan to dance in the parking lot of the Post Exchange? Probably not anytime soon, unless God calls me to do such things. I do plan to celebrate, though. I desire to have David's heart, falling so in love with my Savior, and becoming so thankful for what He's done, that just like those players in the end zone, I can't help but celebrate, regardless of what's going on around me. I desire to have so much praise and joy that my heart overflows and affects everything within reach. That is some kind of celebration.

We can celebrate with cake and streamers, with the radio up as loud as it will go singing praise to our Father, or simply dancing with our kids in the kitchen. Regardless, whether these celebrations are for yardage gained or touchdowns, we need to celebrate. We need to remind ourselves of God's provision, as well as testifying to others of God's work in our lives.

When God instructed the Israelites to celebrate the Passover, it wasn't a one-time shot. He commanded them to continue the celebration annually, even after they entered the Promised Land. This time was not just for them to remember, but to teach future generations and the other nations around them about God's faithfulness and power. We should do the same.

I've thought many times about journaling and keeping an account of what God has done in my life. I would love to hand down such a treasure to my children so they could tangibly grasp God at work from beginning to end. They could see God in my salvation, in His provision when my mom died, in the grace He showed me when I divorced, in the awesome power of love when I married my husband, and in the joy He brought when our children arrived.

They could also witness the little things God had done like preparing homes for us in advance when we moved, churches He led us to where we could serve and be challenged, friends that He's brought to push us further in our faith, and just the joys of everyday, like listening to a two-year-old sing "Jesus Loves Me" from his bedroom.

What an awesome testimony, an awesome legacy, to leave behind. I could fill volumes with the love, grace, and provision of my Savior in my life. We have reason to celebrate, regardless of our current circumstance. We serve a God who is able and a God who is faithful. What more could we ask?

Number 35

The one player I always root for is my husband, number thirty-five on his high school team. I may encourage others, but in the end, he's the one who matters most. While standing on the sidelines, whether during practices or games, I watch intently for just one jersey, "Yates

35." He's my partner. I'd have very little purpose as a cheerleader at this game if it weren't for him.

We've looked at celebration from every angle—celebrating big things, little things, future things, and just the fact that we have an awesome God, but I believe it's important to include our husbands in the party. These celebrations are certainly not for us alone.

In many of our marriages, mine included, we tend to share more about the challenges than the joys. I find myself frequently complaining more than encouraging or celebrating. We use the precious time we have with each other to share some vital information, but we also use a vast amount of that time asking them to do something, sharing the frustrations we have, or rattling off all the things we still need to get done. We rarely take as much time saying thank you or sharing our excitement and joy.

To combat such a trend, my husband and I have attempted to schedule times like date night, periods of time when we focus on each other. Although scheduling this is challenging, we're always thankful that we did. It's provided great opportunities to talk to each other, share our joys, and be thankful for the gift God gave us in each other. In-between these date nights, we try to make time at least once a day to stop and just share with each other, to see what God is doing. We've found that if we don't make time, these opportunities never happen.

Additionally, I've found that I have to make an intentional effort to say thank you to my husband for all he does, and to God, who gave him to me. I know God can see my heart, but I want Him to hear the words, "Thank you, God, for the gift of my husband." I want my husband to hear the same.

I get so caught up in washing clothes and doing dishes, I forget to remind my husband how awesome I truly believe he is. Not perfect, mind you, but perfect for me. I've given him little cards—even tucked them into the backpack he takes to work. I've walked across the room just to hug him, looked him in the face, and told him how thankful I am God gave him to me.

In celebrating the gift of my husband in these moments, I find my heart changes. My frustrations with him for not helping dress children or take out the trash become inconsequential. I remember why I married him, and again become thankful he picked me.

These little celebrations of our marriage are opportunities to celebrate life and all God has done in us and for us. We start seeing a bigger picture of what God would have for us as a team, and are then able to celebrate in anticipation of what He's going to do next. God uses these times to draw us to each other and to Him.

God says to, "rejoice in the wife of your youth" (Proverbs 5:18). I believe that could go both ways. We should also rejoice in the *husband* of our youth. I, personally, plan to keep my eye on number "35," and be forever thankful to my God for the gift.

Bottom line—celebrate and rejoice. From touchdowns to first downs, they're all worthy of a dance. So—do a dance in the end zone, choreographed or not, and celebrate!

Rock on

Standing on the sidelines, we can smell the drops of fatigue and determination. The coolness of the night brings the glare of stadium lights with it, and the band marches off the field to find relief at the concession stand. The missing patches of grass on the field are visual reminders of the battle we've been through and a challenge for what's to come.

The bleachers bustle again with fans anticipating the team's entrance; cowbells are heard as die-hards get antsy for some action. Glancing at the scoreboard, the team takes the field once more, focusing solely on the victory within reach. The cheerleaders, always faithful, jump from the sidelines, pom-poms waving, pulling together the spectators and players into a united front. We will win.

Cheerleaders perform a job no others can do. They're a much anticipated and crucial part of the game, though the game may never be about them. The stunts they perform, both during the game and in competitions of their own, have left us in awe of their athleticism and dedication. They fulfill a number of obligations, and yet they do them all with a proficiency which amazes us. They rock.

Military wives rock, as well. We've battled injury and experienced victory, weathered many storms, and landed phenomenal amounts of stunts. We've survived and conquered—and will do it again. Sustained by the love of a Savior, we've learned to celebrate along the way.

This game for which we cheer is not a game at all, but a real-life adventure we've embraced. We may never receive medals or have our names in the local paper, but the contributions we make are unparalleled. For the most part, we love the assignment we've been given, joyfully making contributions in our communities and our families.

In this military-wife life, we long ago surpassed the infatuation experienced by high school cheerleaders, and have become true professionals in our dedication both to our husbands and our Savior. We've learned to love the job we've been privileged to hold, and we also find joy in the challenge of accomplishing all God has called us to do.

Training daily, celebrating joyfully, and doing what God guides us to do everyday, this is the legacy we should desire to leave behind. Let's grab our pom-poms and get to it. Rock on, chicks!

Epilogue

I love being a military wife. Some days I'm really good at it, and other days I'm not, but I wouldn't trade one day. This military-wife life is exactly where God wants me, and there's no better place to be.

I want to live this life—not just survive. Survival mode is unacceptable. I refuse to sit on the sidelines and wait for a better time or place because I haven't learned to be content where I am. Contentment doesn't equal laziness.

God has marked out a plan for our lives, and I long to joyfully run the race He set for me with everything I have. I desire to have a testimony like Paul's in 2 Timothy when he said, "I have fought the good fight, I have finished the race, I have kept the faith. Now there is in store for me the crown of righteousness, which the Lord, the righteous Judge, will award me on that day—and not only to me, but also to all who have longed for his appearing" (2 Timothy 4:7-8).

God has a plan. His plans are for me to seek Him out daily and to fall so in love with Him that my whole desire in life is to serve Him. I want to give my life as a sacrifice to the Savior who gave everything to me. Strange as it may seem, though, this life doesn't feel like a sacrifice at all, but an opportunity to show my love for Him.

I mess up, frequently. I disappoint myself and most likely disappoint Him, as well. Thankfully, He knows I'm going to mess up, and He loves me anyway. How grateful I am for His unfailing love and amazing grace. I want to finish my race, knowing I gave it everything I had. Leaning into the finish, I can't wait to fall into the arms of my Savior.

Paul completely understood and told the Philippians, "Not that I have already obtained all this, or have already been made perfect, but I press on to take hold of that for which Christ Jesus took hold of me. Brothers, I do not consider myself yet to have taken hold of it. But one thing I do: Forgetting what is behind and straining toward what is ahead, I press on toward the goal to win the prize for which God has called me heavenward in Christ Jesus" (Philippians 3:12-14).

Bottom line: the only way to do more than simply survive this life is to know my Savior personally. Do you know Him?

In order for us to be true followers of Christ, we must first understand **His immeasurable love** for us. Jesus explained this by telling us, "For God so loved the world that he gave his one and only Son, that whoever believes in him shall not perish but have eternal life. For God did not send his Son into the world to condemn the world, but to save the world through him" (John 3:16-17). God loved us so much He sent His only Son to be born as a man and then to die for us.

This had to happen; we need salvation. **We all sin.** Romans 3:23 says, "For all have sinned and fall short of the glory of God." This **sin requires punishment.** According to Romans 6:23, "For the wages of sin is death, but the gift of God is eternal life in Christ Jesus our Lord." In His infinite love, **God paid the price** for our sins through His Son, Jesus. "But God demonstrates his own love for us in this: While we were still sinners, Christ died for us" (Romans 5:8).

Accepting this **free gift of salvation** is easy! Romans 10:9-10 says, "That if you confess with your mouth, 'Jesus is Lord,' and believe in your heart that God raised him from the dead, you will be saved. For it is with your heart that you believe and are justified, and it is with your mouth that you confess and are saved."

Please do not close this book before you have made a decision about where you will spend eternity. This grace is something we could never earn, and yet God offers it to us free of charge. What an awesome gift!

Thank you for joining me on this journey. I long for us all to live the life we have been given with passion and hope. This is my prayer for you:

> For this reason I kneel before the Father, from whom his whole family in heaven and on earth derives its name. I pray that out of his glorious riches he may strengthen you with power through his Spirit in your inner being, so that Christ may dwell in your hearts through faith. And I pray that you, being rooted and established in love, may have power, together with all the saints, to grasp how wide and long and high and deep is the love of Christ, and to know this love surpasses knowledge—that you may be filled to the measure of all the fullness of God. Now to him who is able to do immeasurably more than all we ask or imagine, according to his power that is at work within us, to him be glory in the church and in Christ Jesus throughout all generations, for ever and ever! Amen. (Ephesians 3:14-21)